MONEY DOES GROW ON TREES

THE SIMPLE 7 STEP FINANCIAL PLAN

PETER ZIGGY

Published in 2013 in Australia by Peter Ziggy

ziggy@peterziggy.com

www.peterziggy.com

Book Production: OpenBook Creative

Design: Chantilly Creative

Editor: Cavaletti Communications

Cover illustration: Based on an image from iStockphoto.com/xxx

National Library of Australia Cataloguing-in-Publication entry (pbk)

Author: Ziggy, Peter, author.

Title: Money does grow on trees : the 7 step financial plan / Peter Ziggy.

ISBN: 9780987558695 (paperback)

ISBN: 9780992328306 (ebook : epub)

ISBN::   9780992328313 (ebook : kindle)

Subjects: Wealth--Popular works.

          Finance, Personal--Popular works.

          Financial literacy--Popular works.

Dewey Number: 332.024

Disclaimer: The material in this publication is of the nature of general comment only, and does not represent professional advice. It is not intended to provide specific guidance for particular circumstances and it should not be relied on as the basis for any decision to take action on any matter which it covers. Readers should obtain professional advice where appropriate, before making any such decision. To the maximum extent permitted by law, the author and publisher disclaim all responsibility and liability to any person, arising directly or indirectly from any person taking or not taking action based upon the information in this publication.

Acknowledgements

I'd like to dedicate this book to my kids, Nathan and Naomi. Although I'm writing the book for mums and dads who are not clear on their financial plan, I also am writing it for them.

That way, one day, even if I'm not around, they can look back and be proud of what their dad accomplished and believe that they also can achieve.

I'd like to acknowledge my wife Katina who has been extremely supportive during the whole time of writing, and has backed me in everything I've had a go at. She's been my rock and without her support, I could have never gotten this book done. Love you girl!

Acknowledgements must also go to the team at Cavaletti Communications, particularly Paul Lonerghan who encouraged me almost daily during the whole writing and editing process, mate you pulled me through!

And how could I not include Julie "Jules" Renouf from Open Creative. She and her team took the manuscript and have turned it into something really special. A fabulous book cover, the back blurb, internal design and a heap of other stuff to make it (and me) look good, thank you so much Jules!

This is also for my parents, who as Greek migrants, came out to this great land of Australia to start a better life for them and their children and I bear the fruit of the seed they planted all those years ago. Last but not least I am extremely lucky to have the best brother in the world, Arthur or "Archie" as he mostly prefers, has been my best friend. We connect on so many levels and he just really understands me. Thanks heaps bro.

And I want to acknowledge you, the reader, for taking the time to read this book - I totally believe you will get so much out of it. I want to encourage you to get your finances sorted and get out there, live life and follow your dreams!

Foreword

Having worked in the money industry for over 30 years myself, when Ziggy told me he was going to write a book on financial planning, I must admit I was a little sceptical. Not that I doubted his ability, but I wondered how it would differ from all the many other books out there on the topic, as most are just far too technical and might I say, too boring for the average person to read.

Now that it is written, I have to say, it is a job well done! It offers a refreshing approach on a complex subject, making it easy to understand with lots of practical advice and solid information.

This book is ideal to keep after reading, to use as a resource or reference point, as your circumstances change throughout life.

Many of the pages will cause you to smile, as Peter brings helpful illustrations in a positive and humorous way to a subject that has often only been presented in a technical and complex way.

This book will guide you on a clear pathway with tips on how to go about confidently planning your lifetime financial future.

I understand Ziggy when he says that clients just want to know that they will have enough money to last them and that they are heading in the right direction. However, clients generally don't know where to begin or who to trust and they often don't have the time to do it themselves. I'm pleased to say that this book covers all of these issues.

Lastly and most importantly, the author's humility, integrity, professionalism and commitment to 'walking the talk' give extra credibility to this book's value.

Enjoy the read!

John Sikkema
CEO Halftime Australia – Author of *Enriched Re-defining Wealth*

Table of Contents

'It is not the critic who counts: not the man who points out how the strong man stumbles or where the doer of deeds could have done better. The credit belongs to the man who is actually in the arena, whose face is marred by dust and sweat and blood, who strives valiantly, who errs and comes up short again and again, because there is no effort without error or shortcoming, but who knows the great enthusiasms, the great devotions, who spends himself for a worthy cause; who, at the best, knows, in the end, the triumph of high achievement, and who, at the worst, if he fails, at least he fails while daring greatly, so that his place shall never be with those cold and timid souls who knew neither victory nor defeat.'

Theodore Roosevelt

Introduction

Why do we need this book?

Start with the end in mind and you will plan well. Gone with the Wind recently celebrated its 75th anniversary. It took author Margaret Mitchell 10 years to complete the masterpiece, typing chapter after chapter. But the first chapter she typed was the last chapter of the book. She began with the end in mind. Everything that followed had a purpose.

We all want to retire with a comfortable nest egg. Preferably sooner rather than later. But where do you invest, how do you protect yourself and your cash-flow, and most importantly, how do you find someone whose advice you can trust? Because we've all seen and read the horror stories.

The chances are, you're probably not a financial expert and that's understandable given financial management isn't typically offered in our schools. It should be. It's a fundamental requirement for a successful life.

Most people just want some direction in their finances. They want to know that they are on track (even if they don't know what the track looks like!). You're probably in a similar situation. However, you are confronted with three distinct problems that prevent you from getting on the track:

1. You don't know where to begin
2. You don't know who to speak to and whom to trust
3. You don't have the time to increase your knowledge to do it yourself

Your cash-flow might be strong in gross terms. But the net amount after taxes and expenses? That's often another story, isn't it? I bet you're wondering just where it all goes? I can tell you, if you traced it all back you'd be horrified.

"Okay," I hear you ask, "what can I do about it? After the taxman gets his share and I pay my bills, there's nothing left. I can't even think about investing, so there's no point in seeing a financial planner!"

This situation is hard to handle because we all need holidays, every family should dine out occasionally, and it's a great thing to take your kids to sporting events and to enjoy activities with family and friends. Are you a typical hard working, caring family that just wants to be comfortable?

'Money will buy you a fine dog, but only love can make it wag its tail'
Richard Friedman

During my financial planning career over the last 20 years, I've seen people such as yourself time and again and met lovely people who have a good life, but they are just not totally satisfied with it. Something is just not right financially but you just don't know what to do about it.

Complete the following in your own words in a way that captures your frustrations:

- There is way too much ...
- There aren't enough ...
- I wish I had more ...
- I prefer a little bit less ...
- I get down thinking about ...
- I secretly hate ...
- It ticks me off when ...

Now consider a scenario where things are different:
- In this scenario things are brilliant – because all your finances are sorted, you are investing for your retirement, enjoying holidays, dining out and spending more time doing things that are fun and give you pleasure

- You are feeling great about your future and your children's future
- You don't have to worry about your retirement and having enough
- You are proud of your family and your ability to provide
- You're making a big difference in the lives of other people

You've now uncovered the secret

But best of all, you have uncovered the top secret that most people don't discover. The secret is that this is the time to grow your relationships, spend more time on travelling, dine out more and even do something that will help your community. This is real happiness! You are also able to support your favourite charity and tick off the items in your bucket list (what, you don't have one?). If you were to find such a place as this, then in the words of a famous Guns N' Roses song, you would be in 'Paradise City'.

We only get one life – we might wish for two

DH Lawrence once said:

'If only we could have two lives, the first one in which to make our mistakes and the second one in which to profit from those mistakes.'

Unfortunately there are no dress rehearsals for life – we are on stage straight away. So the question I have for you to ponder is this; how can you make the most of the rest of your life?

Two step process
1. Break with the past

There was a young police officer taking his final exam to get through the program. The first three questions in this exam were relatively easy and then he got to question four. Question four went like this:

"You're on patrol in outer London when an explosion occurs in a gas main in a nearby street. On investigation you find that a large hole has been blown in the footpath and there is an overturned van lying nearby. Inside the van there is a strong smell of alcohol. Both occupants, a man and a woman are injured. You recognise the woman as the wife of your divisional inspector, who is at present away in the USA. A passing motorist stops to offer you assistance but you realise he is a man who is wanted for armed robbery. Suddenly another man runs out of a nearby house shouting that his wife is expecting a baby and that the shock of the explosion has made the birth imminent. Another man is crying for help having been blown into an adjacent canal by the explosion and he cannot swim. Bearing in mind the provisions of *The Mental Health Act*, describe in a few words what actions you would take."

The police officer thought for a moment, picked up his pen and wrote, "I would take off my uniform and mingle with the crowd."

It's so tempting to mingle with the crowd; to become average, to be just someone else, but it's in our blood and our DNA not only to exist but also to prosper, to educate, to deliver, to build and to change.

2. Have the courage to make a new start

Two caterpillars where sitting on a branch when a butterfly flew past – one caterpillar turned to the other and said, "You won't catch me going up in one of those."

Many have a fear of leaving life behind – lots of people resist moving forward and looking forward to much better things!

Don't let your emotions dictate things: you will have ups and downs, you will have negative thoughts that are designed to drag you down – how can you resist this?

How do we achieve the above?

1. Time – devote and allocate time to your goals
2. Prioritise – relationships become very important
3. Communicate with others – get help, feedback, advice and guidance
4. Generous giving – sow into what you want to reap: break with material things, there is joy in giving

Why should we do it?

1. Because there is so much reward and satisfaction to come
2. Because you'll be able to change other people's lives
3. Because you will have money and you can grow money on trees
4. At the end of your life, you can say, "I'm pleased with my life"

A process to make the secret real

In this book I'm going to take you through a four-part series (7 steps in all) on how to make sure you have enough. I want to de-mystify the financial planning industry for you, get you on track and get you some proper advice. Here are the steps:

Step 1. Goals and objectives

You've heard all the phrases such as, "If you aim at nothing, then that's what you'll hit" or "If you fail to plan, then you plan to fail". My favourite is by Stephen Covey who said, "Begin with the end in mind." This section motivates you to start dreaming of some of your activities in retirement.

Step 2. Inefficiencies

We identify areas in your finances that could be more efficient and effective. I will show you how to release cash-flow for further investment and wealth creation.

Step 3. Recommendations

I make specific recommendations and get you thinking about the 'must do's'.

Step 4. Investments

What, when, how and how much.

Step 5. Insurance

An annoying 'must do', but a must do nevertheless; the horror stories I have seen over the years just allow no leeway here. You must be insured. But I show you how to do it efficiently and without feeling ripped off.

Step 6. Cash-flow

This is key to more investment – and it's surprisingly easy to free cash up with some simple manoeuvring.

Step 7. Products

The nitty-gritty.

What made me write this book?

I have had the privilege of working with and advising clients for more than 20 years. And I still love it. To see people come in with what they think is a hopeless situation and to catch up with them years later in a very different place is one of my life's great joys.

As an accountant working with business owners, what I initially saw was that they wanted the financial world explained to them in terms that could be easily understood. My job was made easier because as their accountant, they had a deep trust in me and what stood behind me: my CPA qualification.

Then as I focused more in the financial planning arena people did not seem to be as open or trusting. And even though I had an accounting qualification, the industry had become so tainted that trust had to be earned. And this took time.

The bad advice from planners

I also found that many advisers had a 'one product fits all' approach and were remunerated handsomely by fund managers for recommending their products – rather than what was best for the client. They told clients that, "All this is free for you, the fund manager is paying me." Which was in fact true. However what the client wasn't told was that the fund manager was drawing the funds from their investment and passing it on to the planner.

I have found that there are three types of financial planners:

a) the charlatan financial planner who looks after their own interests

b) the genuine financial planner who wants to do the right thing by the client but his/her lack of technical expertise and experience prohibits them from doing so, and

c) the genuine and honest financial planner who has the technical expertise to put together tax-effective long-term strategies for clients.

The industry certainly needs more of the (c) type adviser. More advisers who are all about strategy and plans rather than products and commissions. More advisers who have their client's best interest at heart and more advisers who are passionate about an industry that helps people achieve their goals and dreams.

I'm hoping this book will help you find this type of adviser and before you even meet with them, you will know where to seek them out and also know the types of things they should be saying to you. Just in case you are dealing with a wolf in sheep's clothing.

Economic bias

Employing a financial planner will likely introduce you to the concept of economic bias. This is the concept where the person you are dealing with has a vested interest in making you follow a certain path – a path that will suit them better, rather than you. For example, when buying a used car, the seller's economic bias is in getting you to pay as much as possible for the car. That's an obvious example and the issue in financial planning is that economic bias is sometimes hard to see. The example is the financial planner who recommends a certain product because it pays him a high commission, not because it necessarily suits your needs. I'll give you a series of questions with which to question your prospective new planner to establish whether he or she has economic bias.

Some facts and making sense of them

Fact 1 – People are living longer today. Experts project that retirees will spend an estimated 20 to 25 years in retirement as life spans continue to increase.

Fact 2 – Even though people are living longer it does not mean we are healthier and health issues affect the capacity to work.

Fact 3 – At a time when people are living longer, workers are expected to provide for their own retirement needs by investing and saving.

Even if you were able to diagnose your own financial situation and craft a strategy, you're then confronted by the mammoth task of literally thousands of investment, insurance and loan options to choose from!

Can I DIY it?

Many give it a go themselves. After all that's part of being an Aussie right? The problem is that even though there are some who have 'had a go' successfully the road is mostly littered with those who made a complete mess of things. In some cases it has cost them their marriage. If this is you, then please be encouraged that there is still time to make up for it; you just need the right advice and I will show you how to get that.

There are financial events throughout your life that have a major impact. Take divorce for example. No one would deny that it's an emotional event of the most powerful sort; however it's also a financial event. And the financial picture changes dramatically.

The unfortunate thing is that most people think financial planning is all about money. When you say that you want financial advice, exactly what type of advice do you expect? Is it advice in shares, insurance, loans and property? Or is it more? Would you like to know how to manage your cash-flow better? Do you want some guidance on budgeting? Or do you just want to know that you are heading in the right direction?

It takes knowledge across the spectrum

Unfortunately, not every financial planner is able to guide you in the right direction and yes; this is a complete indictment on the industry. Dare I say many financial planners don't even know where to begin themselves. And that's not a problem as long as they are upfront about it instead of trying to off-load the latest structured product or managed fund to you.

Free is not free

Some even call themselves financial planners when they are specialists in a particular area. Take the insurance adviser, most of whom are extremely competent. However, insurance is just part of the mix. Perhaps you've ventured online and been attracted to the promise of 'free' advice. If you're the type of person who believes in 'value for money' then what value do you think there might be when there is no money involved?

If you fail to plan...

If you've seen a financial planner, then you've probably been told you need a financial plan. Why do you need a financial plan? The main reason is you need to plan your life so that in retirement you have absolutely nothing to do with the government. You don't want to have to rely on the aged pension and if you do, that usually means you're not going to have enough for a decent retirement. There are great strategies around social security, but with our changing demographics, you really can't rely on it being in a form you'll like when you get there. And trust me, you don't want to spend your morning at the Centrelink office trying to sort out some administration cock-up!

Cash-flow is your engine room

The topic of money comes under many guises in books and various journals, whether it's referred to under the topics of wealth creation, property, shares, financial independence and even in psychology books telling you how to program your mind for money! Ultimately it all comes back to cash-flow and whether you have enough of it. I will show you how to do this.

Stuff happens

Just when many people recently thought their lives were on track, the Global Financial Crisis (GFC) came along and people planning on retirement found themselves working for much longer. Unfortunately for them, from 2007 until now we have had the deepest global recession since the Great Depression and question marks still remain as to whether we are in fact coming out of it.

"Will I have enough?" is a question that covers many financial aspects:

- Will I have enough in retirement?
- Will I have enough if my spouse dies?
- Will I have enough if through sickness or accident I can't work for three months, three years or ever again?
- Will I have enough if I lose my job?
- Will I have enough if the school fees keep going up?
- Will I have enough if every single cost continues to rise?

How much is enough?

No matter what you have, it's never enough.

For the purposes of this book let me give you a simple definition in the context of retirement. You will have enough if the total investment assets you have (property, shares and cash) generate enough cash-flow (notice I didn't use the word 'income') to fund your lifestyle (either the one you've imposed upon yourself over time or the one you aspire to).

And don't forget your 'bucket list'

Let's cut straight to the chase. Here are the questions you need to answer, in order to start planning. Because when you know where you want to go, planning the route that gets you there is the easy part.

- What do you want to do in retirement?

List the activities you'd enjoy, things you want to learn or places you'd like to visit during retirement. What do you see yourself doing daily, monthly or yearly? How might these activities differ in the first 10 years of retirement, the second 10 years and beyond?

- Where do you want to live?

Answering this question will help you to estimate the living expenses you'll need to cover as part of your plan.

- What does retirement mean to you?

Some people imagine living in retirement as a time to rebalance priorities, spend time with family, enjoy a hobby or give back to the community – what about you?

- What does financial security mean to you?

What do you need to be comfortable in your retirement – lifetime income strategies, funds to cover possible risks, the ability to leave a legacy?

- What are the risks to pursuing your goals?

What concerns you about retirement? What would you do to address risks that you may face? Your financial plan will incorporate ways to manage risks including longevity, legacy, market, inflation and taxes, health care and long-term care.

- How will you pay for the retirement you want?

How much money will you need to be able to live the life you imagine? What assets and resources might be available to support your retirement? What income streams can you plan for that will cover your fixed expenses as well as any discretionary spending?

Wait, there's more

Considering these questions and visualising the specifics of your retirement will help you better understand the elements you need to plan for and the costs that may be involved. Don't hesitate to discuss your thoughts with others to hear their points of view – this will encourage friends and family in their retirement planning and help you get ideas you might want to apply to yours.

If you have a spouse or partner, be sure to talk about how your lives might change during retirement – as individuals and as a couple – by considering questions such as:

- What does the change from working to not working mean to you?
- How will you fill the time that you previously devoted to your work and commute?
- What does your day look like?
- What will you do together and apart during retirement?
- How will it feel to live a retirement lifestyle?
- Is it time to leave your partner and REALLY enjoy life in retirement? ... only joking

Consider giving your desired retirement a test drive by spending one or two weeks doing what you would plan to do once you retire.

Don't marry for money; you can borrow it cheaper.

SCOTTISH PROVERB

CHAPTER 1:
Money As A Tool

Money is not valuable per se – it's just paper and bits of metal. Its value lies in what it enables us to do. Money is freedom. Money facilitates transactions and relationships, lets us share time with friends and family and gives us the wherewithal to pursue dreams.

Money and its uses and needs can be broken up into three areas:

1. Raising kids

According to the *May 2013 AMP.NATSEM Income and Wealth Report: Prices these days! The cost of living in Australia*, the cost of raising kids is on the rise. A typical middle-income family will spend around $812,000 to raise two children, up by 50% on 2007 figures when it cost around $537,000.

Can you believe there has been such a large increase in just five years? That's 50% or $275,000 in just five years! What about other living costs?

2. Living

The *AMP.NATSEM Income and Wealth Report: Prices these days! The cost of living in Australia* explores how living costs have changed since 1984 finding that average income growth more than covered the cost of living over this period.

However, everyday essentials including electricity increased 253%, rent prices grew 223%, mortgages increased 256%, petrol increased 208% and public transport costs jumped 287%. In other words, "Life is bloody expensive!"

3. Retirement savings

Ultimately, you will live the life you can afford. So if you think that you are going to need more you're going to need to save more, earn more, win the lottery, inherit lots of money or rob a bank.

Clearly, the one constant for every Australian in retirement is meeting basic living costs. Thanks to a ground-breaking study originally released in February 2004 and now updated every few months or so, I can tell you, with some authority, how much money you need to live on each year in retirement, depending on the lifestyle that you want to have. The study, known as the 'ASFA Retirement Standard', measures the cost of a modest or comfortable lifestyle in retirement, in dollar terms, and adjusts these costs periodically in line with the cost of living.

The ASFA Retirement Standard study is groundbreaking because Australians now have a tangible savings target with a clear idea of what type of lifestyle that amount of money can give them in retirement.

Assuming you own your own home, you need the following amounts of money, after tax, to give a single person, or a couple, a basic, modest or comfortable lifestyle (as at May 2013):

Basic Lifestyle – Age pension only – $21,018 a year for a single person, or $31,689 for a couple (this represents 27.7% of Male Total Average Weekly Earnings. Are you willing to live on 27.7% of an average Australian's income?).

Modest Lifestyle – $22,641 a year, or $32,603 for a couple – Receiving an after-tax income that is slightly higher than the age pension obviously gives you a better lifestyle than living solely on social security, but you can only afford low-cost activities.

Comfortable lifestyle – ($41,169 a year, or $56,317 for a couple) – Living on this level of after-tax income means you can enjoy more recreational activities. Also, you can afford to purchase private health insurance, higher quality household goods and travel regularly. Even so, a 'comfortable' lifestyle isn't outlandish.

Some other highlights from the research

1. We're spending more on discretionary items
Households are spending a greater portion of income on private schooling, restaurants, childcare and tertiary education. Between 30 and 40 per cent of household income is spent on basic necessities.

2. Incomes have outpaced the cost of living across the board since 1984
Households, on average, are $224 per week better off than in 1984. (Why doesn't it feel like it?)

3. The cost of services has increased strongly since the 1980s
And increased very 'strongly' in the last three to four years! Interestingly the report says that medical, dental and insurance costs have risen faster than private school fees (shhh... don't tell the private schools).

4. Work demands have driven increases in childcare spending
Given women are encouraged to remain in the workforce whilst having children, it's no surprise that childcare spending has gone up. Childcare centres all over the country are full, with long waiting lists.

5. Australia's petrol prices are among the lowest in the world
At current prices of around $1.40 we're very low. Compare this to water. I still can't believe I get asked to pay $2.50 for 250mls of bottled water and can get a litre (1,000mls) of petrol for $1.40 even though it has to be dug out of the ground. Which one is the rip off?

6. Sydney continues to be the most expensive city to live in but both Sydney and Melbourne are two of the most expensive cities in the world.

Summary

- Households today are more focused on lifestyle
- Many Australians are leading busier lives and facing greater demands on their time
- Households are spending more on education, holidays and eating out
- Australia currently has one of the highest standards of living in the world

The bad news is that the report The *AMP.NATSEM Income and Wealth Report: Prices these days! The cost of living in Australia* confirms what has generally been known for some time and that is people are not allowing any spending for investment, that is, they are not providing for retirement.

The good news I read into this report is that we don't lack in gross income but rather in net income so that's something your financial planner can work on with you. After all, "It's not what you make it's what you keep."

An oil sheik says in a gallery:

'I really admire Picasso. There is nobody who was able to sell oil so expensive.'

CHAPTER 2:
Avoid The
Poverty Trap

According to Webster's dictionary, the definition of poverty is: "the condition of being poor, or not having enough to live on." The poverty trap is "any self-reinforcing mechanism which causes poverty to persist." Refer to the diagram on the right.

Now, thank God that we don't live in poverty in Australia, however in financial planning terms there are many people caught in the poverty trap. Let me introduce this concept by explaining the stages it occurs in.

Stage 1
When you're in your early 20s life is good. Given you are single and earning a good income your cash-flow is strong but your cash is spent on working, dining out and travelling and nothing is left for investment.

Stage 2
Then just when you're thinking you are happy, you do something silly and get married! You buy your first house and even though you're both working, most of the money is going to your mortgage, plus you're still dining out and doing some travelling before the kids come along.

Stage 3
Then you decide to start a family and your net cash-flow really falls away as you convert to a single income and have all the obligations of mortgage payments, education costs, family expenses and some travelling. And this is after the taxman has got his share. So there is certainly no surplus income for investment in this stage of your life!

Stage 4

The kids leave home; the home loan is significantly reduced or even paid off. And just when your cash-flow begins to increase, you realise that you are 55 or 60 and there is very little time left for investment. I still get clients during this stage who ask me for advice and all I can say is that it's certainly better late than never and something is still salvageable.

Stage 5

Enjoy retirement! If you have any money left that is.

The Poverty Trap

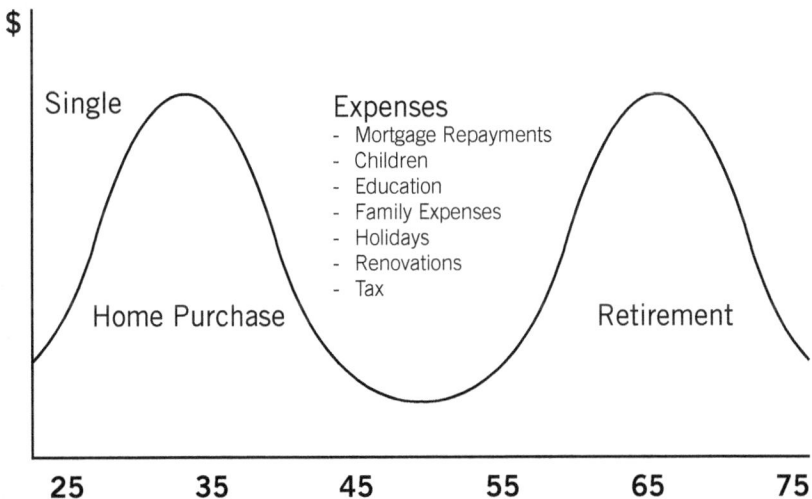

Your priorities will determine if you achieve your goals. 90% of retirees have worse cashflow in retirement than in their early 20s!

PART 1

WHERE TO BEGIN?

'Too many people spend money they haven't earned,
to buy things they don't want, to impress people they don't like.'
Will Smith

The longest journey starts with just a footstep – or so says an ancient Chinese proverb. And the same is true of your journey into financial independence – in whatever form that takes.

This section of the book will help you create the platform your wealth will stand upon. I want you to think through a few things, I want you to understand some of the basic jargon and I want to help you choose the financial planner who is right for you.

Choosing the right planner is crucial. There has been much made of planners who work for large institutions who simply push that institution's products at the expense of products that may be better suited to the client. We've all read the stories of horrendously inappropriate products being foisted upon people – because of the high commissions the planner receives. So choosing a planner is crucial and I'll give you a 10-question template that will help you source the best planner for you.

This section will look at what you want to achieve, and how to do it in a way that sits comfortably with you.

- Goals and objectives – so what do you really want?
- Risk profile – shall we play poker?
- Selecting an adviser – who are these creepy people?
- Dealing with inefficiencies – I've got a leak!

What leads most people into debt?

Trying to catch up with people who are already there.

CHAPTER 3: Goals and objectives

When I first meet up with a client I ask the golden question, "What are your goals and objectives?" and inevitably, the answer (after a long blank stare) is, "Well, I've never really given it much thought".

I bet, just like me, you're always thinking about your financial situation, your future and how your life story may read in years to come. I bet, just like me, you would really love to be doing a whole range of things right now that have nothing to do with work.

So if I was to ask you about your goals and objectives, could you answer me? If the answer is 'Yes', then well done thy good and faithful servant! If not, just let me say you have had goals and objectives all your life and in fact you are in the process of implementing some of them right now. Let me also say that goals are a complete waste of time. Let me explain.

Our goals and objectives can be broken down into three main areas:
1. Our responsibilities
2. Our worries
3. Our dreams

These can be further broken down:
Our responsibilities
a) Educating my children
b) Supporting my family
c) Minimising my taxes (yes this should be everyone's responsibility)

Our worries
a) Protecting my family if I'm not around
b) Maintaining my lifestyle
c) Having enough for retirement

Our dreams

    a) Working because I want to not because I have to

    b) Pursuing my hobbies and passions and ticking off bucket list items

    c) Being generous to favourite charities, and making a difference in the world

You do have some good objectives!

So if I was to ask you again about your goals and objectives you could now give me a great answer, right? You're obviously already doing many of the above items, particularly when it comes to your responsibilities – and for that I congratulate you! You're probably already quite focused on part a) and b) of your responsibilities – maybe without recognising just how properly responsible that makes you. What I am really trying to achieve with this book is you being able to identify all your worries, deal with them by working with a competent financial planner and then setting about pursuing your dreams. That's where all the fun and action is!

Let me share something with you about my passions. My passions are my God (don't worry, I'm not going to get all religious on you) and my family. I love being a financial planner as I get to be involved in your passions as well. I have a passion for helping people deal with their worries successfully, but my biggest passion for clients is to see them live out their dreams. I'm all about fun! It's time to write out a bucket list, put some objectives in place and plan the ultimate prize – a great, well-funded future! And the best part of all? It's quite simple.

Let's stop thinking and start doing. Let's get really specific about what it is you want and be determined to do whatever it takes. Have those objectives front and centre of your mind.

Why goals are a complete waste of time

Remember when I said that goals were a complete waste of time? I'm sure you think I'm a little crazy, but let me explain by defining and differentiating between a goal and an objective as these two words are used interchangeably – and incorrectly – today.

MEANING

Goal – The purpose toward which an endeavour is directed.

Objective – Something that one's efforts or actions are intended to attain or accomplish; a purpose; a target.

EXAMPLE

Goal – I want to **achieve** success in the field of monogenic research and do what no-one has ever done.

Objective – I want to **complete** this thesis on genetic research by the end of this year.

ACTION

Goal – Generic action, with an outcome we strive towards.

Objective – Specific action – the objective supports attainment of the associated goal.

MEASURE

Goals may not be strictly measurable or tangible.

Objectives on the other hand **must** be measurable and tangible.

TIMEFRAME

Goals – Short to medium-term.

Objectives – Longer term.

Have short-term goals and long-term objectives

So I exaggerated to make a point – goals are not a complete waste of time but can you see how much more powerful an objective over a goal is? This is a really important distinction to make. Whilst goals can be hazy if you don't deliberately make them a little smarter; objectives have clear outcomes. Incorporate this into your thinking and I promise you, your chances of achieving all the things you want to achieve in life (including financial security) will improve out of sight.

Right thinking leads to right speaking leads to right doing … right?

So to recap, goals are broad and objectives are smart.

Make your goals SMART

Most people find it difficult to articulate their objectives and tend to break them up into short, medium and long-term objectives.

Deciding on your financial objectives is an important first step in reaching them. To achieve short to medium-term goals, it's helpful to turn them into SMART goals. SMART goals are: *Specific, Measurable, Attainable, Realistic* and *Time-bound.*

For example, let's say one of your medium-term goals is to take your family to Bali over the summer holidays. Here's how to make it a SMART goal.

Specific: A specific goal is, "I want to spend summer holidays in Bali with my family." A vague goal, by comparison, would be, "I want to do something fun over the summer holidays."

Measurable: You need $3,500 for flights and accommodation for the trip to Bali including food for the week. This is more concrete than, "I need money for the trip."

Attainable: You have about six months in which to save for your trip and you'll save the money from your partner's income. You'll need to save $600 per month, or $70 per week to go on the trip. You are more likely to see results with this goal than if you say, "I'll save any money that's left over at the end of the month."

Realistic: You and your family will leave on the Thursday night and return on the following Sunday afternoon. A vague goal is something like, "We'll make it a ten-day trip."

Time-bound: You'll have 75 percent of the money saved by September. A vague goal would be "I'll have the money by early spring."

This is just one example of a SMART goal. As your life continues, try to think of how you can apply this SMART goal-setting approach to future short, medium and long-term goals.

Examples of these types of goals could be as follows:

Short-term
1. **Debt reduction.** Most people tend to have multiple forms of debt in the form of credit cards, personal loans and property loans. Paying these down should be a top priority. Focus on the debt that has the highest interest rate first, as it will cost you the most money over time.

2. **Emergency fund.** Be prepared for the unexpected. Try to have a minimum of three months' worth of living expenses in the bank or at least available to access via some sort of facility.

3. **Spend less than you earn.** Seems fairly logical but if you want to learn to manage your money well, develop the habit of spending less than you earn. A generous credit card limit is not extra earnings!

A second life habit is to learn to pay yourself first, which means routinely putting a little bit of every pay packet into savings or investment.

4. Transportation. Consider public transport as a cost-effective alternative to commuting to work by car. It will save you the cost of car payments, car insurance, petrol, oil, maintenance, parking fees and tolls. If public transportation is not a viable option, consider buying a reliable used vehicle to meet transportation needs. A wise man once said buy the cheapest car your ego will let you drive.

Medium-term
1. Getting married/starting a family. Weddings can range in cost from relatively little to tens of thousands of dollars, particularly if you're Greek and have a large and extended family like mine (we had around 480 people at my wedding!). Remember that you can use money that you don't spend on a wedding for other things in your budget or on your list of goals. As a couple, you and your spouse will share costs that each of you previously paid individually – rent, utilities, groceries, etc. – so living expenses generally go down. Put the savings towards a shared financial goal.

2. Saving for a home. To buy a home, you'll probably need a deposit of around 20 percent of the home's purchase price. For instance, on a $600,000 home, you'd make a payment of around $120,000.

3. Saving for retirement. Although retirement may still be 20 to 25 years away, starting now to invest small amounts of money consistently over time will add up to bigger overall savings in the future.

Long-term
1. Saving for children's education. You'll have to make a decision on whether to send your children to a local government school, a semi-pri-

vate school (such as Catholic school) or a private school. Unless you send them to a government school your school fees will be substantial, particularly if you are sending them to private school from primary school age. Having a savings and investment strategy in advance is crucial for a private school objective.

2. Caring for parents. As you age so too will your parents. They may need some financial help from you at some stage in their life, particularly if serious illness strikes or they require extended assisted living or nursing home care.

So what are your objectives? Take some time now to work out what you want to accomplish:

1. Within the next year
2. Within the next 3 to 5 years
3. Within the next 5 to 10 years

The first step in achieving goals is to decide what they are – and then write them down so they are real. Once you write them down, stick them on your wall, your refrigerator, or some other highly visible place so that you are constantly reminded of what you are working towards. Get the kids involved and have some common goals that you can all work together for. Not only does this teach them how to set financial goals for themselves, but what a great family bond you create!

What's the best way to get in touch with your long-lost relatives?

Win the Lottery.

CHAPTER 4:
Risk profile

"The art is not in making money, but in keeping it."
Proverb

Once you've selected a financial planner he or she will have plenty of questions for you. These questions will relate to your objectives and he or she will have specific questions about income, assets and liabilities.

Another set of questions that you will need to answer (usually by way of questionnaire) relates to your risk profile. All investors have differing attitudes toward risk. When it comes to investing, it is important to consider your risk profile or tolerance carefully, including how comfortable you are with the possibility of losing money, or that returns on your investment could vary widely from year to year.

Understanding your personal risk tolerance will help you choose an appropriate asset allocation. The following points and questions are similar to those that your financial planner will ask. Have some fun and answer them now so that you can give truly considered answers when the time comes. The idea of them is to help you to determine the investment mix that's appropriate for your needs.

Know yourself through your investment experience

How would you describe your investment experience and understanding of financial markets?

Which of the following applies to you:
- You just started investing in the last year
- You understand the basics of investing
- You have been investing on your own for several years and are reasonably confident of your knowledge of financial markets
- Your knowledge of financial markets is well above average and you make investment decisions confidently

Risk tolerance – what you're comfortable with

To establish an investment strategy that you will be comfortable with, you need to consider the possibility that the value of your investment may decline even though this may be temporary. Are you prepared to accept the possibility of a negative return at any time in exchange for potentially higher long-term returns? What percentage of your money would you be prepared to invest in higher-risk investments?

Which of the following is important to you:

- Avoiding any short-term losses
- Receiving regular income from investments
- Long-term growth in the value of investments
- Protection against inflation

In October 1987 the stock market fell more than 20 per cent in one day. If you owned an investment that fell by 20 per cent in a short time what would you do?

- Sell all of the remaining investment (Conservative)
- Sell a portion of the remaining investment (Conservative to Balanced)
- Hold the investment and sell nothing (Balanced or Aggressive)
- Buy more of the investment (Aggressive)

Investment goals and objectives

Why are you investing? Is it for something in the near future (new car, or deposit on a home) or something further off (a young child's education or your own retirement)? If your investing goals are short-term, you'll want your money to be there – with interest – when you need it. Therefore you need to focus on relatively short-term investments like term deposits or a cash management trust. If, on the other hand, you are investing for the long-term, you may be able to afford to take some risk in pursuit of a higher return. Shares and property, which have historically provided higher returns than fixed interest or cash over time, may be more appropriate.

Investment timeframe

When do you expect to access all or part of your investments?
- Less than 1 year (immediate access)
- Less than 2 years (short-term)
- 2 to 5 years (short to mid-term)
- 6 to 10 Years (mid to long-term)
- Over 10 Years (long-term)

Liquidity / cash requirements

How much money do you need to keep available for emergencies such as house repairs, a dental emergency or serious car repairs? These emergencies can be a serious setback if you are not prepared. The amount of your emergency fund will depend on your current lifestyle and expenses. As a general rule you should have about three months of income set aside to meet emergencies without needing to rely on credit cards. A cash management trust that pays high interest can be a good place to keep emergency funds. If you have a loan, however, the more effective strategy is to have the funds sitting against it in either an offset facility or in the loan itself, ready and available to be withdrawn when needed (remember only for emergencies – and holidays don't classify as an emergency!).

Age and income

Your age and your income – particularly the stability of your income – are important factors to consider when determining your investment profile. If you are young you can afford to take a longer-term view and any short-term losses may have minimal effect. If your income or employment is unstable you will need to take this into account when setting your investment goals.

A word of warning

Grand plans for retirement may not be achievable if you have a conservative risk profile. Bear in mind that maybe you won't be able to achieve all your objectives in life unless your investments engage in a little risk in return for higher returns. I'm not suggesting you don't have dreams (in fact I encourage that), but you need to be realistic.

Risk vs Return

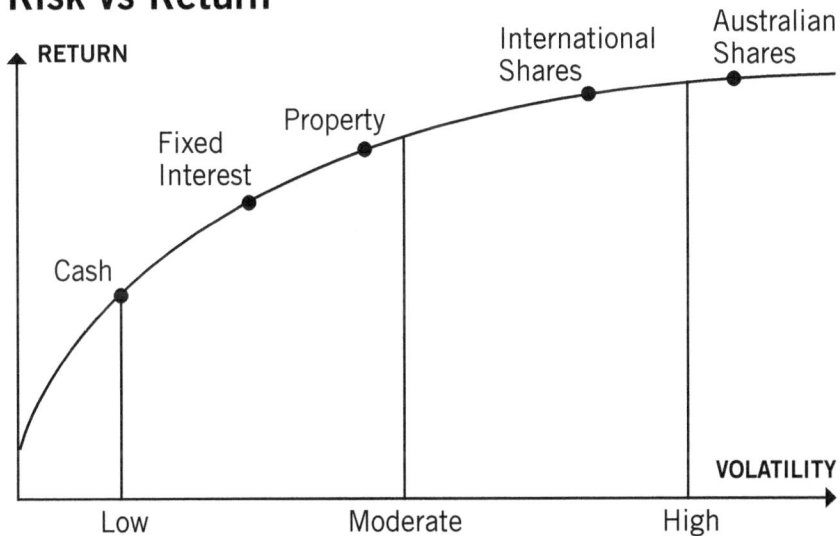

Risk is the **uncertainty** that an investment will earn its expected rate of return. Therefore as the risk increases so does the uncertainty in the expected rate of return (which also increases). However, when there is a return in such a case then that return is *higher* than the expected rate of return. Double Dutch? All you really need to understand is that the greater return you seek, the greater risk you need to take.

Summary

Here are the different risk profile types:

Conservative
Your primary investment goal is capital protection. You require stable growth and/or a high level of income, and access to your investment within three years.

Cautious
Your primary investment goal is capital protection. Investors in this risk profile require fairly stable growth and/or a moderate level of income. Your investment term is three years or more.

Moderate
Your primary investment goal is capital growth. You can tolerate some fluctuations in the value of your investment in anticipation of a higher return. You don't require an income and you are prepared to invest for five years or more.

Moderately aggressive
Your primary investment goal is capital growth. Investors in this risk profile can tolerate a fair level of fluctuation in the value of the investment in anticipation of possible higher returns. You don't require an income and you are prepared to invest for five to 10 years.

Aggressive
Your primary investment goal is long-term capital growth. You can tolerate substantial fluctuation in the value of your investment in the short-term in anticipation of the highest possible return over a period of 10 years or more.

Q: How to make a million in the stock market?

A: Start with two!

CHAPTER 5:
Selecting an advisor

It may surprise you to learn that not all advisers can give you holistic advice encompassing the range of your financial needs. An insurance adviser, for example, will likely give excellent life insurance advice, but not good investment advice. Some advisers will suggest investments that pay them the best commission, rather than investments that best suit your needs.

You will normally consider help from a financial planner for a number of reasons, whether it's deciding to upgrade to a new home, planning for retirement, or your children's education. Whatever your needs, working with a financial planner can be a helpful step in securing your financial future.

A good adviser will help you become financially secure

Financial advice helps you make decisions about your money. Good advice from an experienced, well-informed financial adviser can help you become more financially secure. Financial planning can be quite complex. There are many rules and regulations and it is hard to keep up-to-date on legislation and the diverse range of financial services products available. Most people lack the experience and know-how to manage their finances effectively, not to mention the time to do it properly. Just as you would see a lawyer for their specialist legal advice I highly recommend you engage the services of a financial planner to help you reach your financial goals.

Look for someone who can help you on a long-term basis

You want to find a financial adviser with the experience and knowledge to give you the level of service you're looking for. You also want someone who can develop a strategy to reach your financial goals and can provide a broad range of investment choices. Avoid people limited to 'selling' one investment product or solution regardless of your needs.

Get to know your adviser

Do as much research as possible before choosing a financial adviser. Below is a list of questions that will help you interview and evaluate several financial planners to find the one that's right for you. A good strategy is to search on the web for advisers close to you, look at their websites, including the 'About Us' and shortlist three who you are initially comfortable with. Then arrange to meet with each and assess them using the questions below. You will want to select a competent, qualified professional with whom you feel comfortable, and one whose business style suits your financial planning needs.

Aim for broad skills plus a specialty

It's my recommendation that you find an adviser who has a broad knowledge in all areas financial with a specialty in one area, for example Self Managed Super Funds. Broadly speaking, the adviser, or at least his business should be able to cover the following services:

- goal setting
- tax planning
- estate planning
- insurance planning
- business planning
- retirement planning
- education planning
- investment planning and review

Your financial planner will help you map out a plan for your short and long-term financial needs. A good financial plan will include the following:

- an outline of your financial position and needs
- set out your goals
- clearly explain a strategy for achieving your goals
- discuss risk and how to deal with it
- recommend investments to manage your money effectively
- demonstrate how each investment will help you reach your goals
- explain and detail the commissions and benefits your financial planner will receive

Once your financial plan is in place:

- review it annually
- keep track of your investments
- tell your adviser about major changes in your circumstances (retrenchment, new baby, retirement etc.)
- make sure that any changes to your plan are communicated to you in writing and you understand the changes before agreeing.

A good planner is strategic

Above all you want a financial planner who is strategic and provides strategic advice. By way of comparison, if you walked in to see your doctor and told him you were sick, the last thing you want is a quick prescription and no analysis! Prescription without diagnosis is malpractice! What you expect is for him to ask enough questions about your symptoms so he can provide you with a diagnosis. Once the diagnosis is made the doctor will develop a strategy and treatment plan. Medication would be just one part of the plan.

In the same way, when you see a financial planner, the last thing you need is to be sold a product upfront. The planner needs to find out what the core issues are, put together a strategy, and then recommend the appropriate products to fit that strategy. Do you see the difference? You will generally get a good gut feel when you meet the right planner. And your planner will get a good feel for you as a client as well. I recall years ago a couple came to me after being referred by their accountant, as they were not totally satisfied with their financial planner at the time. After an hour's discussion, the wife said, "You've made more sense in an hour than our current planner has made in eight years!" That certainly made me feel good, however it also scared me to think there are financial planners out there who are just not making sense to their clients.

10 QUESTIONS TO ASK A FINANCIAL PLANNER

Q1. WHAT EXPERIENCE DO YOU HAVE?

Find out how long the planner has been in practice and the number and types of companies with which he/she has been associated. Ask the planner to briefly describe their work experience and how it relates to their current practice. Choose a financial planner who has experience in counseling individuals on their financial needs.

Q2. WHAT ARE YOUR QUALIFICATIONS?

Many financial professionals use the term 'financial planner'. Ask the planner what qualifies them to offer financial planning advice and whether he/she is recognised as a CFP® (Certified Financial Planner). If not, why not? You wouldn't accept a junior doctor performing knee surgery on you so why would you accept anything less than the most qualified and experienced adviser you can get – after all, you're trusting them with your private financial affairs.

Q3. WHO IS YOUR DEALER GROUP?

The dealer group is the entity that holds the major license with the Australian Securities & Investment Commission (ASIC) and then provides the financial planner with the authority to begin work with clients as an Authorised Representative. The Dealer Group will make a decision on the planner's services based on their knowledge and competency and they are ultimately responsible for the recommendations made. You really want to know if they are aligned to just one institution such as an insurance company or a bank. This is crucial because you don't want advice based on just that bank or insurance company's products. Is it product selling first and foremost? Or is it about you and your needs? A clue is whether they address those needs by providing fee for service, or are they paid on commission by the dealer group?

Q4. WHAT SERVICES DO YOU OFFER?

The services a financial planner offers depends on a number of factors including credentials, licenses and areas of expertise. The list of services (among other things) is set out in their Financial Services Guide (FSG), which must be given to you at the first meeting or soon after. Planners can only provide services listed in their FSG. Generally, financial planners cannot recommend insurance or securities products such as shares without the proper licenses, or give investment advice unless they are an Authorised Representative of a Dealer Group, which holds the license with ASIC. The Dealer Group is ultimately responsible for the advice being given to you.

Q5. WHAT TYPE OF CLIENTS DO YOU HAVE?

Ask the financial planner about the type of clients and financial situations they typically like to work with. Some planners prefer to develop one overall plan by bringing together all of your financial goals. Others provide advice on specific areas, as needed. Make sure the planner's viewpoint on investing is not too cautious or overly aggressive for you. Some planners require you to have a certain net worth before offering services. Find out if the planner will carry out the financial recommendations developed for you or refer you to others who will do so.

Q6. WILL YOU BE THE ONLY PERSON WORKING WITH ME?

The financial planner may work with you themself or have others in the office assist them. You may want to meet everyone who will be working with you. If the planner works with outside professionals (such as lawyers, insurance agents or tax specialists) to develop or carry out financial planning recommendations, get a list of their names to check on their backgrounds.

Q7. HOW WILL I PAY FOR YOUR SERVICES?

As part of your financial planning agreement, the financial planner should clearly tell you in writing how they will be paid for the services to be provided.

Planners can be paid in several ways:
- A salary paid by the company for which the planner works. The planner's employer receives payment from you or others, either in fees or commissions, in order to pay the planner's salary.
- Fees based on an hourly rate, a flat rate, or on a percentage of your assets and/or income.
- Commissions paid by a third party from the products sold to you to carry out the financial planning recommendations such as insurance.
- A combination of fees and commissions, whereby fees are charged for the amount of work done to develop financial planning recommendations and commissions are received from any products sold. In addition, some planners may offset some portion of the fees you pay if they receive commissions for carrying out their recommendations.

PS, Please note, although upfront and on-going commissions have been banned on new investment products from 1 July 2013, the rules do not apply to insurance.

Q8. HOW MUCH DO YOU TYPICALLY CHARGE?

While the amount you pay the planner will depend on your particular needs, the financial planner should be able to provide you with an estimate of possible costs based on the work to be performed. Such costs should include the planner's hourly rates or flat fees or the percentage he would receive as commission on products you may purchase as part of the financial planning recommendations.

By way of guideline, a full and comprehensive financial plan (that covers all the issues mentioned in this book) will be worth $3,500 to $7,500. A financial plan that covers one or two specific areas would be much less, usually less than $1,500.

Q9. COULD ANYONE BESIDES ME BENEFIT FROM YOUR RECOMMENDATIONS?

Some business relationships or partnerships that a planner has could affect their professional judgement while working with you, inhibiting the planner from acting in your best interest. Ask the planner to provide you with a description of his/her conflicts of interest in writing. For example, financial planners who sell insurance policies, securities or managed funds may have a business relationship with the companies that provide these financial products. The planner may also have relationships or partnerships that should be disclosed to you; such as business or commissions he/she receives for referring you to an insurance agent, accountant or a lawyer for implementation of planning suggestions. All of this really should be disclosed by the planner anyway but I encourage you to still ask the question.

Q10. HAVE YOU EVER BEEN PUBLICLY DISCIPLINED FOR ANY UNLAWFUL OR UNETHICAL ACTIONS IN YOUR PROFESSIONAL CAREER?

Several government and professional regulatory organisations, such as ASIC or the Financial Planning Association keep records on the disciplinary history of financial planners. Ask what organisations the planner is regulated by and contact these groups to conduct a background check. All licensed financial planners are registered with ASIC and you can quite easily conduct a search on their site at www.asic.gov.au.

If you think no one
cares about you,
try missing a couple
of loan payments.

CHAPTER 6:
Inefficiencies

Inefficiencies refer to areas in your financial affairs that are not major but need attending to sooner rather than later as they can have a big impact on your cash-flow and take your planning off the beaten track.

Let me give you an example. You notice a small oil leak in the car and mentally note it needs to be attended to. If you get it looked at in the next month or so, chances are it's just a small crack somewhere, which is easily rectified. If you leave it for too long, chances are it turns into something big, with a possible breakdown on the freeway and all sorts of big costs and frustrating inconvenience.

Small issues in your financial affairs that could turn nasty are:

- Loans – you may have a loan product that is not appropriate for you or you don't have a competitive interest rate
- Insurance – you may be over-insured or have doubled up on level of cover with multiple policies and are wasting cash-flow
- Property – you may be holding properties that are a massive drain on your cash-flow because of high body corporate fees or poor sinking fund
- Tax – you may be paying too much tax which can be easily minimised with appropriate structures

Summary

- You need short-term goals and long-term objectives

- Your financial objectives are in three parts – responsibilities, worries, dreams

- Your goals should be SMART – Specific, Measurable, Attainable, Realistic and Time-bound

- Understand your risk profile – this will decide your investment options

- More risk does often mean more reward – but are you comfortable?

- Is your planner independent? Use the 10 Questions to help you decide

- Take care of the niggling small stuff now – don't leave it

PART 2

HOW TO KNOW
WHAT'S BEST

"An economist is an expert who will know tomorrow why the things he predicted yesterday didn't happen today."
Author Unknown....but repeated by many!

This section takes you for a ride on the knowledge train! You work at whatever you do and you know a lot of the 'inside' secrets of your industry, correct? This section will give a look at some of the 'inside' secrets of the financial industry. It's not actually secret, it's just that most people don't know the details – so I'm going to explain it in, hopefully, plain English.

Here's what we'll cover:

- Recommendations – what type of advice should I expect?
- Investments – why this one over that one?
- Insurance – I'm going along just fine thanks!

If robbers ever broke into my house and searched for money I'd just laugh and search with them.

CHAPTER 7:
Recommendations

You will usually go to an adviser for advice. I know that sounds obvious but you'd be amazed how many people walk into an adviser's office to get advice and walk out with a product, and probably no idea what it's designed to do. Oh sure the adviser gave them a 'Statement of Advice' but it's not exactly in plain English. It gives information on the product and lists all the 'risks' involved. Oh yes and it also states somewhere at the back the amount of money the adviser is going to earn.

But is the recommended product appropriate for you? Was the advice given in your best interests? Well that's entirely a different story.

New legislation protects us all

On 1 July 2013 legislation changed to ensure that financial planners give advice that is in the best interest of the client. This is known as having a fiduciary duty to the client. Previously the planner only had to show that a product was 'appropriate for you' which, needless to say, does not mean it was in your best interests. Thank God for these changes. In accounting you always have a fiduciary duty to your client and this was ingrained in me from my early days since I graduated in 1993.

Now I'm not suggesting that planners in the past were making recommendations that were not in the client's best interests... ahh, who am I kidding? Of course that's what I'm saying, otherwise there would not have been a need for the change!

The 'appropriate' get-out-of-jail clause

How did it used to work? Take this scenario. A financial planner has two different products that he/she can recommend – Product A and Product B. Both products are 'appropriate' for you but only Product B is in your 'best interests', yet you were recommended Product A. How so?

If the planner was to receive an incentive or some additional 'benefit' to recommend Product A and it fitted the criteria of 'appropriate' then which product do you think you would have ended up with?

And sadly, that's what happened to many people. This change was long overdue and the net effect for you will be better financial arrangements – if you find the right planner. Because that's what it now comes down to – planners who can understand your needs, have a vast knowledge of all the products that are out there and can apply them to your situation.

Two sorts of advice

There are two issues here when it comes to 'advice'. There is strategic advice and there is product advice. Let me explain by way of example and throw in some Greek flavour.

Nikos (39) and Athinoula (35) have a lovely home worth $550,000 but with two children and another one on the way, they really need to upgrade. The loan on their current home is currently $185,000 and they believe they would need to spend $700,000 on a larger home. Nikos works in his souvlaki van and Athinoula is a successful designer. They have worked out they have $1,700 surplus per month. They have a small portfolio of shares, which they set up a few years ago for the long-term and their super is locked away.

What they want to know is a) How can they afford to upgrade their home, and b) Should they sell their shares to help fund it? They are concerned that if they sell their shares they get rid of the one decent asset that they had originally planned for retirement.

What Nikos and Athinoula need, amongst many other things, is a strategic plan that will model a few scenario cash-flows and ultimately show them the most effective and efficient strategy.

They DO NOT need another product. They DO NOT need another flogging from an adviser who recommends something that is in his/her interests! They need strategic advice that helps them achieve their goal of a new home.

What type of recommendations should you expect?

The services offered by a financial planner

The financial planning services you will require will depend on your specific financial goals and circumstances. A financial planner can offer you general assistance and direction across all financial markets or specialise in areas such as:

Taxation
- tax planning
- salary packaging / salary sacrifice
- superannuation
- estate planning and trusts

Investments
- managed investments
- share market (direct investments)
- securities and futures markets
- property
- cash or fixed interest
- superannuation
- margin lending or gearing

Insurance
- life insurance
- income protection
- health

General
- budgeting
- estate planning
- retirement planning
- debt and risk management

Some important things to note:

It amazes me that the majority of financial planners do not give any recommendations when it comes to property investment. Effectively there are only two real asset classes that provide growth over the long term – property and shares. So how can you ignore one out of the two asset classes? Australians are big on property, so I just don't understand why property is not really considered by many planners. Actually, I lie because I do understand. It's because the large institutions such as banks are not in the business of selling property so their financial planners only recommend products they make money from.

There are some financial planners (non-bank planners) who do make property recommendations but are not allowed to model it into your financial plan and have to be quiet about it. I wonder why.

A few other things to note:

- Never make a cheque for an investment payable to your adviser and never transfer money across to the adviser's account. Money invested should always be made out to the third party product you are investing in or put into a trust account.
- Be wary of planners who seem to offer their services 'free of charge' – you can be sure you will be paying for it elsewhere.

- Check the fine print. You should receive three key disclosure documents from your financial planner:
  - o Financial Services Guide (FSG) – document to help you evaluate whether to obtain the services of the financial planning firm.
  - o Statement of Advice (SOA) – outlines the advice you are receiving.
  - o Product Disclosure Statement (PDS) – outlines the details of the financial products you are being recommended.
- Don't always go for the cheapest provider and ensure that what you invest is relative to what you pay for.
- Take extreme care with high rates of return. Ask your financial adviser to provide a written explanation with the risks fully explained before committing.

Cooling off periods. You generally get a 14-day 'cooling off' period if you purchase managed funds, life insurance, super or general insurance.

The safest way
to double your
money is to fold it
over and put it in
your pocket.

KIN HUBBARD

CHAPTER 8:
Investments

When did this notion of investments begin? Well my friend, in the words of Lipps Inc (1980) and Pseudo Echo (1986) let me take you back to funky town … or are YOU meant to take me to funky town? Anyway, in around 1700 BC the Code of Hammurabi provided a legalframework for investment, establishing a means for the pledge of collateral by codifying debtor and creditor rights in regard to pledged land. We have followed this rough framework to a certain extent even today.

What is speculation?

In the early 1900s purchasers of stocks, bonds and other securities were described in the media, academia and commerce as speculators. By the 1950s, the term 'investment' had come to denote the more conservative end of the securities spectrum, while speculation was applied by financial brokers and their advertising agencies to higher risk securities much in vogue at that time. Since the last half of the twentieth century, the terms 'speculation' and 'speculator' have specifically referred to higher risk ventures.

The different meaning of 'investment'

Investment has different meanings in finance and economics. In economics, investment refers to saving and deferring consumption. Investment is involved in many areas of the economy, such as business management and finance whether for households, firms or governments.

In finance, investment is putting money into something with the expectation of gain, usually over a longer term. This may or may not be backed by research and analysis. Most or all forms of investment involve some form of risk, such as investment in shares, property and even fixed interest securities which are subject, amongst other things, to inflation risk. By this I mean that if your money is simply earning interest and the bank will simply give you the amount invested back at the end of the term deposit, then you've run the risk of your money now being able to buy less than it used to because of inflation.

Short-term gambling

In contrast, putting money into something with a hope of short-term gain, without thorough analysis, is gambling or speculation. I include here the purchase of shares in the hope of a short-term gain without any intention of holding them for the long-term. (Time is your friend in the stock market!)

Income always follows assets so when it comes to retirement it's extremely important to hold quality assets that produce income.

Investments are often made indirectly through intermediaries, such as fund managers, banks or brokers. These institutions may pool money received from a large number of individuals into funds such as investment trusts or unit trusts to make large-scale investments. Each individual investor then has an indirect or direct claim on the assets purchased, subject to charges levied by the intermediary, which may be large and varied. It generally does not include deposits with a bank or similar institution. Investment usually involves diversification of assets in order to avoid unnecessary and unproductive risk.

In Australia we love property and we love to tell others that we purchased an "investment property". It's much sexier than saying "I bought shares" or "I bought some fixed interest securities".

Investment types

Broadly speaking, there are four main types of investments available in the Australian marketplace:

- Cash and fixed interest investments
- Bonds
- Property
- Shares

Cash and fixed interest investments

Cash investments are the most common form of investment in Australia, encompassing products such as bank accounts, term deposits and cash management trusts.

The appeal is that they provide easy access to your money when you need it, and there's no chance you could lose any capital – so they're very secure.

However, they usually provide very little income and no capital growth. So they can actually be quite risky over the long-term because inflation eats away at the value of your investment.

For most investors, these products are suitable for:

- use as a transaction account
- keeping cash on hand for short-term expenses and emergencies
- short-term savings where you cannot afford any risk to your capital

Bonds

Bonds are a loan made to either a government or a corporate organisation – you 'loan' your money for a set amount of time at a predetermined interest rate (either a fixed rate or at a fixed level above a variable rate) and receive a steady income stream through regular interest payments.

Bonds can be traded at prices that reflect prevailing interest rates. At the end of the term, you receive a payment equal to the bond's face value.

Whilst bonds generally provide a more attractive return than cash, they do carry higher risk. The price of a bond rises as interest rates fall, and falls as interest rates rise. The price rises because you're now getting more money in comparison to the prevailing interest rate at the bank. It falls because your investment is now paying less than the comparatively safer bank interest rate. If interest rates rise sufficiently, it is possible to obtain a negative investment return.

Bonds are generally suited to investors who are seeking a higher return than is available from cash, but who are still seeking a low risk investment.

Shares

Shares (also known as equities or stocks) represent ownership in a company. When you buy a share, you become a part owner in the company and become entitled to share in its future value and profits.

Shares offer growth to investors in two key ways:

1. As the overall value of the company increases, the value of your shares also increases.
2. Companies can also elect to pay part of their profits to shareholders as an income payment, rather than reinvesting all profits back into the company. These income payments are known as 'dividends'.

The tax effectiveness of dividends

One of the major advantages of dividends is that they can be very tax effective. If you invest in an Australian company that has already paid tax on its profits, tax credits (known as franking credits) may be attached to the dividends the company pays to you. These franking credits can be used to offset tax payable by you on other income. In other words, you've already paid tax (via your ownership of the company) so you're not expected to pay it twice, or indeed any more than you should, so the government credits you. In addition, shares held for more than 12 months qualify for a 50 per cent discount on any capital gains tax payable.

As shares are simply little parcels of companies, they have the potential to generate very high investment returns. However, they also have the potential to fall in value if the company's performance falters.

Shares are generally best suited to investors who:

- want to build up a solid nest egg for medium and long-term savings goals
- have a longer investment timeframe (5 to 7 years +)
- are comfortable with some volatility in their investment value over the short-term, in exchange for higher returns over the long-term.

Property

Property is one asset class that most Australians are already very familiar with. Property investment offers value to investors in two ways:

1. Properties increase in capital value over time as house and land prices rise.
2. You earn rental income from your tenants.

Like shares, property prices fluctuate and have periods of sustained high returns and sustained low returns, so property is generally only suitable as a long-term investment.

Property is generally best suited to investors who:

- don't require 'emergency' access to their money
- have a long-term investment timeframe (5 to 7 years +)
- have the ability to meet mortgage repayments in the event that interest rates rise or if there is difficulty finding tenants.

Some alternative investments

An alternative investment is an investment product other than the traditional investments of shares, bonds, cash or property. The term is a relatively loose one and includes tangible assets such as precious metals, art, wine, antiques, coins or stamps and some financial assets such as commodities, private equity, hedge funds, carbon credits, venture capital, forests/timber, film production and financial derivatives.

The simple explanation

Let's use an example to demonstrate the types of investments. For instance, pretend you're in a Charlie Brown cartoon and are going to start a lemonade stand.

You need some money to get your stand started. You ask your grandmother to lend you $100 and write this down on a piece of paper: "Nan, I owe you (IOU) $100 and I will pay you back in one year plus 5% interest. Love, Tom."

Your grandmother just bought a bond (IOU) by lending money to your 'company' named Dickinson Enterprises Pty Ltd. To get more money, you sell half of your company for $50 to your brother Ben. You put this transaction in writing: "Tom will issue 100 shares of stock. Ben will buy 50 shares for $50. Ben just bought 50% of the shares from Tom."

You sell $500 worth of lemonade. Business is good. Your costs for raw materials and setting up the stand are $150, plus you pay yourself $100 for the hours you work. The company makes profits of $250.

At the end of the year you pay back your grandmother $100 plus $5 interest from the profits. You pay $20 to the shareholders (or owners) which is Ben and yourself. This is called a dividend. You decide to put your dividend money back in the bank. Banking the money is a short-term investment.

This example covers three types of investments: short-term investments, bonds and shares.

Investment risk

Understanding investment risk is the key to developing a successful investment plan. There are three main types of investment risk:

- Permanent loss of capital
- Fluctuating returns
- Not achieving your goals

Every investment has these risks, but all three can be managed.

It's okay to worry, but not too much

Understanding investment risk is the key to developing a successful investment plan. While every investment has potential risks, they can be managed and minimised.

Everybody worries about risk. By getting the right guidance you can keep risk in perspective and identify the types of risk that are acceptable to you and those that are best avoided.

Permanent loss of capital

This is the risk that you probably fear most – the thought of losing all of your money. This might generate most of the newspaper headlines, but in reality it's rare and the risk most easily avoided.

The key is to buy only quality investments and a little of each so that if one does fail, it will only have a small effect on your overall portfolio.

So, should you accept the risk of permanent loss? Are the rewards worth the risk? The answer is yes and no.

No, you shouldn't accept the risk of loss of capital associated with poor quality investments. The risk is too high, and the rewards are often illusory. Good advice from your adviser is crucial here. But yes, you should consider accepting the risk of loss of capital associated with high quality investments. You can balance your portfolio in a way to minimise risk while enjoying the potential good returns. A good adviser will show you how with the help of a diversification strategy.

Fluctuating returns

All investments suffer from fluctuating returns at one time or another.

The asset class which fluctuates the most is shares; their values can change on a minute-by-minute basis. Even over longer timeframes, share returns can fluctuate strongly. And the trouble is we hear about this volatility every night on the news!

What you need to know is good quality investments will go up more often than they go down. In so doing, they will reward you with a superior return over time. As Graph 1 highlights, despite short-term volatility, the value of the Australian share market has increased substantially over the past 60 years.

History of the Australian Sharemarket

January 1900 – June 2010

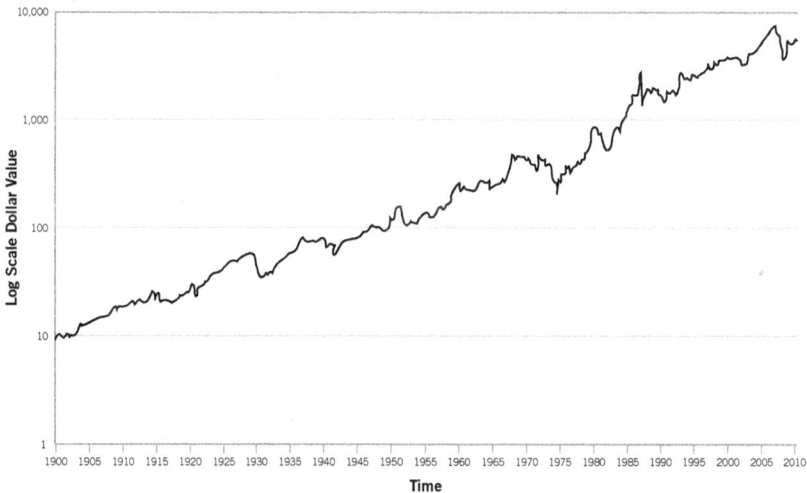

Source: MLC Investments
Commercial & Industrial Index Monthly Averages (1875–1936)
Sydney All Ordinaries Index Monthly Averages (1937–1979)
All Ordinaries Share Price Index Monthly Averages (1980–1999)
All Ordinaries Share Price Index Month End Price (2000–2009)

You can minimise fluctuating returns by:

- investing in quality investments
- investing for the long-term
- diversifying your investments

Diversifying your investments spreads risk and enhances reward

Here's the key: spread the risk for consistent rewards. Risk is part of investing. You can't avoid it, but you can manage it. Diversification is one of these strategies, and generations of investors have used it to reduce investment risk.

Diversification involves spreading your money across a range of different investments. How and what will depend on your goals, the amount of time you have available to invest and the amount of investment risk you're comfortable with.

Diversification is important because every type of investment has its ups and downs. Owning a diverse range of investments should help you achieve smoother, more consistent investment returns over time.

The more ways you diversify, the more you can potentially reduce your risk. For example, you can invest:

- across different asset classes (e.g. cash, fixed interest, property and shares)
- in more than one investment within each type (e.g. invest in several different industries and companies when investing in shares)
- in more than one type of fund, and more than one fund manager, when investing in managed funds
- inside and outside superannuation.

Your timeframe will help determine what you invest in

Short-term – 'parking' cash in a term deposit; for example, housing proceeds where you've sold your home and moved in with your parents while you build the home of your dreams. You want the cash readily available and you can't risk it on the short-term volatility of the stock market.

Medium-term – for example, you're saving for school fees that will start in three years time and go for 12 years or more.

Long-term – retirement funds that you'll access in ten years or so. You can afford a little risk maybe as the funds aren't required in the short-term.

The risk of not achieving your goals

This is the risk of investing in things that don't generate a sufficient return in order for them to meet your financial goals. It typically occurs when you decide to 'play it safe' by investing in cash and term deposits to ensure that you don't lose capital.

However, this can sometimes lead to a worse fate – not having enough money to achieve your goals. After inflation and tax earnings from cash and fixed interests do not really grow your wealth pool. You really need to be investing in property and shares. The income and cap-ital value generated from these two asset classes outperforms all other asset classes over the long term.

'Money is the opposite of the weather. Nobody talks about it, but everybody does something about it.'

REBECCA JOHNSON

CHAPTER 9:
Insurance

Insurance is known in the industry as Risk Management and whilst this sounds fanciful it's actually very accurate. One of the key aspects of financial planning is all about identifying your risks, then calculating them, quantifying them and managing them. The basic principle of insurance is to return the insured to the situation they were in prior to the 'event' to the greatest practical extent.

Before we get into some of the details around the different types of insurance, let me take you back in time and explain how the newest form of insurance began – Trauma (Recovery) insurance.

Dr Marius Barnard's success story

Dr Marius Barnard is the less well known of the two brothers who pioneered heart transplant surgery in 1967 – Marius removed the deceased's heart in one theatre, while Christiaan transplanted it into the living patient waiting in the other theatre. Together they pioneered their radical new ideas and achieved the success we're all aware of today.

A doctor invents Trauma insurance

Dr Barnard's ideas didn't just revolve around medicine. He was also the creator of trauma insurance. When he was interviewed about his original idea for trauma insurance, his story never changed: he saw too much grief and angst among his patients, caused by their physical survival – thanks to modern medicine – coupled with their financial stress (and even ruin) as they had no claim on life insurance, but were still unable to earn an income, or struggled to do so in the face of extreme physical disability. The financial stress of survival worked against everything he was trying to accomplish as a doctor to secure each patient's recovery.

Dr Barnard had a long-standing relationship with the insurance industry as many specialist doctors do. He fought for this new concept, which became known as 'dread disease' insurance, against many odds, not the least of which was the actuarial challenge of pricing a product that no statistics existed for. In the end, he won, as have all the thousands (possibly millions) of insurance claimants since.

Overall Dr Marius Barnard should be very proud of what he achieved over 25 years ago.

Trauma protection – the real family story

The critical thing about trauma insurance is that often it isn't the insured person who directly 'benefits' the most. Oddly, that's a concept that rarely seems to be communicated. Many advisers say to clients, "You say you don't need it and you're probably right – but your family does!"

If Mum gets breast cancer (and it's a 1 in 8 chance these days), then Dad will inevitably want to be around her, while still looking after the children's emotional well being. In many cases there will be little choice and Dad will not be able to afford to simply walk away from his job or business. Trauma insurance may well allow him to do just that while not needing to be concerned about the short-term financial consequences.

Even if Dad can manage that, the last thing he will want to do – or expect the children to do – will be mundane tasks like housework. Yet, in addition to the presence of the family to support her, it may be that a serene, clean and settled environment will contribute to Mum's recovery process. Certainly as she will be in the house 24/7 for some time to come. It is conceivable that the children may well appreciate this more given that both parents can be there, together, at this difficult time.

Trauma really does happen and it can be dramatic

Let's say it isn't Mum. It may be (and statistically it could well be) that Dad although exercising regularly has a heart attack and has to decide whether to keep working as hard as he has been after he recovers. His decision will be dictated to a large degree by the family pressuring him to take it a little slower; in the belief that his work ethic and commitment contributed to his heart attack. This may mean that he has to re-evaluate his role at work.

Dramatic though these scenarios may seem, they are the 'classic' claim stories most planners come across. They are the most common claims, and they happen as much to 40-somethings as to 60-somethings.

A real-life scenario

Around eight years ago, a single mother with three children was referred to me wanting a financial plan. She was a professional earning a reasonable amount of money and wanted to ensure that her and her family's future was well planned for. As part of the plan I recommended insurances be put in place for family protection.

Not less than two years after the insurances were all set up; the client calls me to say that she had a minor car accident. A car had hit her from behind and because she suffered some whiplash, she was taken to hospital where x-rays and other tests were conducted. While she suffered no lasting effects from the accident, the tests showed she had a growth in her neck and it turned out to be thyroid cancer.

She had a decent mortgage, was working hard and putting all three children through private schooling and was now faced with this. Thankfully, she had listened to all my recommendations and had implemented the appropriate level of insurance cover for her. She received a $220,000 trauma pay out which paid out her home loan and let her focus on recovery from the surgery to remove the tumour.

Not all employers are this good

Thankfully she was only off work for six weeks and her employer supported her by paying out her sick leave and letting her remain off work without taking any annual leave. Not all employers are able to provide that level of support (this was a big pharmaceutical company). But even if they hadn't, the income protection was ready to kick in if she made a claim for it (which she didn't need to as it turned out).

She made a full recovery and went back to work. She is still a client today and a very good friend.

At a time like that, there are enough stresses and worries about your illness to also have to worry about financial stress. So let's look at what insurance is and the different types.

What is risk management?

A well-constructed financial plan has two parts – wealth creation and wealth preservation. Wealth creation is designed to build and preserve capital based on the assumption that you will have continued good health and live to a certain age. Wealth preservation, on the other hand, is transferring the risk to another party in the event that something may happen that will prevent you from meeting your long-term financial and lifestyle objectives.

Wealth preservation is known as personal insurance and, in short, it's about ensuring that your assets and resources are protected. Personal insurance is a simple means of transferring risks from individuals who cannot afford to retain the risks, to insurers who can.

Why have personal insurance?

Personal insurance management is important to relieve you and your family of the financial burdens associated with the loss of income if an event occurs. An event like death or permanent/temporary disablement in your prime working years can be devastating for all the family, not just the person affected. Insurance provides peace of mind that you and your family are financially secure by providing an on-going income, debt repayment, a replacement housekeeper/nanny while your children are young and possible funds to meet your children's future education needs.

Why should a professional assess your personal insurance needs?

Given the complex nature of risk management, professional assistance should be enlisted to ensure that the correct type and amount of insurance is established. The type and amount of personal insurance will depend upon your personal financial circumstances and objectives, lifestyle needs, number of dependants and your age.

What types of insurance are available?

The types of insurance policies available are:

- term life insurance
- total and permanent disability
- income protection, and
- trauma insurance.

Life insurance

Life insurance provides financial protection in the event of death and the cost of the insurance depends on the type of cover selected. A regular review of your cover is necessary to ensure you are not under or over-insured.

In determining the most appropriate policy, a balance must be achieved between affordability and the most favourable policy conditions. To determine the amount of cover required, the following considerations are important:

1. current levels of assets and liabilities, especially the amount outstanding under a mortgage on the family home
2. income required to maintain your family's standard of living
3. costs of a housekeeper, day care etc., should these services need to be provided
4. costs of caring for a totally and permanently disabled person.

Life insurance such as term insurance is usually taken out to repay debts (mortgage for example), to cover dependants from the loss of an income provider and/or to secure a business.

Total and Permanent Disability (TPD)
TPD is an additional cover to death cover and it is designed to provide a lump sum should you suffer an illness or injury which totally and permanently incapacitates you and prevents you from working again. TPD can be taken out to repay debts, to cover capital gains tax liabilities and to cover dependants from the loss of an income provider.

Before purchasing a TPD contract, you should establish the circumstances under which the insurance company will pay a claim, as the precise definition of TPD and the conditions that must be met to receive compensation vary considerably with different companies. This is where an expert adviser is crucial.

Income Protection
An income protection policy will pay you income in the event of being unable to work due to illness or injury. Income protection insurance replaces up to 75 per cent of your monthly income for a period up to the policy anniversary date prior to your 65th birthday.

Income protection provides quality cover and a variety of additional features to give added protection and to help you get back on your feet in the event of a claim. The premiums you pay on this type of policy are tax deductible, and the income payments received under the policy will be assessable income for tax purposes.

Trauma insurance
Trauma insurance is a lump sum payment for those who suffer a specified traumatic event such as the diagnosis of cancer, coronary disease, etc. The specific purpose of this is to provide for medical treatment, child care and debt management.

The benefit on a trauma policy is paid to you when the diagnosis is confirmed, not when you die of the condition. This is important because it provides you and your family with a lump sum to use at your discretion, when it is most needed. It may be needed to pay for additional medical care, or perhaps to pay the mortgage to relieve the financial pressure on the household.

Without cover the financial implications of an event can be dreadful. With advancements in medical technology and techniques, patients increasingly have a much better chance of surviving conditions that previously may have been fatal, for example, heart attacks, strokes and malignant cancers.

As existing types of insurance cover (death, total and permanent disability and income protection) did not necessarily cover these types of conditions, the concept of critical illness insurance was introduced.

Ill health can happen to anyone

You should also recognise what our modern lifestyle does to us. You have probably read health articles that say that the cause of many medical conditions today is stress. Stress can produce all kinds of imbalances in your body. It can cause you to age prematurely, give you rashes, cause gastric pains and even hinder fertility. To put it succinctly, stress kills!

Why should you read and understand the contract?

When you take out insurance cover you should obtain the policy contract and read it thoroughly to ensure you understand exactly what the policy is insuring you against. If you are unsure about any aspect of the contract, ask your financial planner to explain anything that you do not understand. This will help you avoid any complications that may arise if you or your estate should need to make a claim on the policy.

Why participate in on-going reviews?

As your wealth grows as a result of the implementation of your financial plan and your personal circumstances change, your need for insurance cover may decline or increase over time. Therefore, it is beneficial to periodically review your insurance cover.

The rise of direct life insurance

These days on TV it seems to me that every second or third commercial is either a sports betting advertisement or a direct insurance advertisement. Usually you'll see a lot of direct selling during daytime TV programs.

I offer a word of warning if you're thinking of purchasing insurance directly this way. I understand that it may seem an easier process, that it can all be done over the phone and that you don't need to see a financial planner. But...

Here are a few reasons for using a financial planner and not going direct:

1. There are subtle differences between insurance products. For example, with income protection – you want to endeavour to lock in an 'agreed' benefit contract. This means you not only want to make sure that you are medically but also financially underwritten at application stage to secure 'agreed' income protection benefits.

2. Many of the direct life insurance policies have many exclusions because the less underwriting that gets done, the more exclusions there need to be on the product to keep the risk pool the same. Will you be covered for everything you think you're covered for? Will you get the money when you need it? Who will help you at claim time?

3. One size does not fit all. Given the myriad of products out there, it is your financial planner who will recommend a product that is suitable for you and in your best interests. And certainly at claim time it's your planner who can provide valuable support and assistance to you.

Summary

- Advisers must now deliver advice in your best interests by law

- Two types of advice – strategic and product-based

- A good planner will advise on tax, investing, insurance and other advice specific to you

- All investments are risky, but you can minimise risk by diversifying

- Investments can be made in cash, bonds, shares or property

- Your time horizon will dictate the asset class you invest in

- Insurance helps you manage risk to you and your family

- Stuff happens and there is insurance now for many things

- Life insurance lets your family carry on

- Trauma and income protection covers let you carry on

- Be wary of direct insurance from TV ads – there are many exclusions

PART 3

HOW DO I KNOW WHERE TO INVEST?

"A bank is a place that will lend you money
if you can prove that you don't need it."
Bob Hope

There are two facets to this; making the money and knowing how to invest it. You can't have one without the other! Hopefully by now I've shown you how valuable a financial planner can be in the structuring process. Earning the money is all very well, but you don't want to waste it with inappropriate structures and nor do you want the possibility of losing it to an event beyond your control. (Yes, another pitch for insurance!)

Borrow money
from pessimists,
they don't expect
it back

CHAPTER 10:
Cash-flow

Most people don't like talking about cash-flow and budgeting, particularly with their financial planner as it usually means that spending needs to be reduced substantially. Not always the case. More often than not I find many clients have strong cash-flow but simply aren't managing it well. Generally, with some simple tinkering, money can be allocated in a much more effective and efficient way to achieve all your goals, both current and future.

People don't like talking about budgets full stop. I don't refer to them as budgets anymore as that gives the perception of constraint. Now I'm not saying spend, spend, spend; in fact I preach to clients that they certainly should live within their means. A budget should really be called an investment plan as I believe every item on it is an investment in your future well being.

Restructuring is the key

Just in the last twelve months I had a couple with a young family and a strong gross income. They couldn't work out why there wasn't the amount of excess cash there should have been. After a full review, I was able to come up with a strategy that saved them enough money to fund another investment property, while reducing their home loan and, most importantly, retaining the lifestyle they wanted with their children.

Efficient allocation

Now I could cover some cash saving tips such as saving money on groceries, utilities, clothing, entertainment etc. but the internet can give you dozens of free budgeting planners and tools. As a financial planner my role is not so much to review every item within your budget (although I would if asked to) but rather assess and review whether there is a more efficient way of allocating your resources. And generally there is. The secret is two-fold; sensible budgeting and proper structures.

Cash-flow is king

Before you can even talk about some budgeting (or investing) you first need to work out what your cash-flow situation is like. In two questions (maximum three) I can find out whether you are in a positive cash-flow situation or a negative one. In other words, what is the change in your net assets over a twelve-month period? Make sense? No? Then speak to your financial planner about putting your financials into a Balance Sheet so you can see it in black and white. I won't cover it here but it is an easy process and one that you can cover in a lot of detail with your planner.

Timing is everything

Sometimes there is an event that can cause a seemingly healthy family cash-flow to fail spectacularly. Sometimes timing is everything. The same is true in personal finance. You may be counting on a big raise, a large commission cheque, or simply your weekly pay cheque and decide to purchase some extras with the understanding that you'll pay off your credit card as the bill comes due.

If everything doesn't proceed according to plan – and isn't it amazing how often it doesn't – you could be left with a cash-flow problem that can either cost you in finance charges or potentially cause you to go bankrupt.

Ziggy's tips to protect cash-flow

What leads most people into debt? Trying to catch up with people who are already there.

So how do we avoid this problem? Let's look at some ways to prevent ever having to deal with a cash-flow crunch.

- Setup monthly payment plans wherever possible, e.g. insurance premiums and utilities
- Identify expenses that could blow out or potentially cause problems such as renovations or legal fees in a dispute
- Keep a close eye on account balances. You'd be amazed how loans can creep up and how cash balances can drop just by simple, but regular, ATM withdrawals
- Make sure you have a cash-flow buffer

Know your finances

Everyone's cash-flow situation is different. Some of us receive a regular salary, while others have irregular income and expenses that make it much more difficult to figure out how to manage your money. The key is to have a firm grasp on your unique cash-flow challenges and have a plan in place for avoiding the dreaded cash-flow crunch. Know it in your head, check balances weekly, understand where cash is going.

Once you have a strategy in place and are now allocating resources to investment, for example an investment property, as well as your usual lifestyle expenses, take the time to ask your adviser to model it for you and recommend alternatives so that you can ensure you can afford it.

Buffer 'insurance'

You should also allow a buffer for unexpected events. Make sure you allow for interest rate fluctuations. My suggestion is use an interest rate of 2% above the prevailing average rate at the time. That will allow for up to four interest rate rises, which is as about as much as you can plan for.

Even if you have a view on interest rates, my suggestion is don't lock it in, as the rate is usually 1-2% higher than the variable rate at the time. So for a period of time you are paying higher rates. Even if rates were to rise up to your fixed rate and you're now par with the market, you're still behind given you've been paying higher rates for a period of time. It is only when rates go up another 1-2% and stay there that you will begin to save... and these are scenarios that even professional economists get wrong – particularly a couple of years out.

My suggestion to clients is to leave loans at the variable rate and allow for a buffer as mentioned in your planning. The reason is you want flexibility in your loan structures. For example, if a great investment property opportunity came up then you really want to have the flexibility to refinance in order to secure the property. You don't want to pay any penalty interest to exit a loan arrangement unless, of course, you think the banks aren't making enough money.

Daddy, how much does it cost to get married?

I don't know, son, I'm still paying for it!

CHAPTER 11:
Products

'Why did God create share analysts?
In order to make weather forecasters look good.'

This is where the rubber meets the road. No one can predict which products will make you the most money over the longer term. You can certainly look at history and make a judgement as to what asset class will grow more, but individual product guesses are just that – guesses. The key here is your risk profile and your timeframe.

So, last but not least are the products. However there is a reason they are last in the process. Let me give you an example. Say you went to the doctor with severe pains in your abdomen. Just as you began to explain to the doctor what the pains felt like, he writes out a prescription and says, "Take two of these daily until the bottle is complete and you'll be fine." "But doctor," you say, "you haven't even asked me where the pain is, what it feels like or how long I've had it?"

In the same way, a financial adviser is being irresponsible to give you a product without understanding what your needs are. Usually you have a strategic problem, and that means you need some quality strategic advice. Then, and only then, are you ready to consider what type of product will fit into your investment strategy. If you hear anything different to that process make sure you run right out of the adviser's office, dust blowing off your sandals on the way out and make sure you grab a few of the 50c chocolates they have from the boxes at reception!

How do you know which product suits you?

How do you understand the product? And if your adviser can't really explain it, again – run! Think back to the CDO (Collateralized Debt Obligation) products. These were investment vehicles consisting of income-producing assets financed by issuing multiple classes of debt and equity. Did that make sense? Don't worry you're not alone. These caused such strife in the GFC – most advisers didn't fully understand them either (and nor, apparently, did the ratings agencies). Highly structured products are best avoided unless you understand them, or your adviser does – and you trust that he or she does.

The questions to ask yourself when listening to your adviser's recommendations are as follows: Is there a hidden agenda, is there a bias, does he/she get more commission for recommending one over the other? Does a larger institution own the adviser's business and are they pushing you to one of the institution's products? Sure, the institution's product may be a perfectly valid option, but makes sure it's not the only choice. If your adviser is constantly pushing the one institution's line of products then something is wrong.

The Approved Product List

Financial planners can only recommend investment products that are on the Dealer Group's Approved Product List (APL). The Dealer Group is the one with the full licence, which then gives authority to the financial planner to practice. The Dealer Group is ultimately responsible for any advice given or any product recommended.

This is your protection that someone with half a brain at least has assessed the products on offer and judged them to be appropriate for clients. Ensure you get a copy of the APL and make sure that all products recommended are on there. It goes without saying that you should not be investing in anything that is not on that list.

Which product is for you?

There are literally thousands of financial products out there so how do you know which one is suitable for you?

A good financial planner will be able to take you through the process from beginning to end. From giving good, solid and sound financial advice, to recommending products that are suitable to your circumstances. Just because a particular product is good, or rated highly by a research company does not necessarily mean it's the best product for you. This is where the skill and knowledge of the financial planner plays a part and, in particular, the planner's knowledge of your personal situation and how to marry this up with the thousands of products out there.

I would recommend that the financial planner you use is non-aligned, meaning that an insurance company or major institution does not own them. This will ensure (hopefully) that you are recommended a product that is just right for your personal situation and not what the large institution is pushing down through their planners.

The end result

The ideal end result of a personal financial plan is one that is geared towards your best interests – not the profitability of the institution a non-independent adviser works for. There are several independent firms available and it's this independence that should give you the confidence and trust you need to have in an adviser.

It's up to you

Financial plans and products can be complex; so good advice from a professional who intimately understand the products and your goals is vital. It won't be free – but we all know free advice is worth what you pay for it.

PART 4

WHAT ELSE SHOULD YOU CONSIDER?

Hopefully by now you're convinced that you need to plan for a financial future, and that failing to plan will get you nowhere. Your first steps are to get the basics done – like establishing cash-flow, establishing an investment plan, working out your insurance coverage and bedding it all down. Once it's in place, you can just sit back and relax... but, as comfortable as you now are, there are a couple of other things you probably need to think about. That's what this chapter is all about – the other things you need to consider.

Priorities

We all understand the principle of, "So much to do but so little time to do it in." I bet the same applies in your finances. What to do, where to focus, how to decide?

Should you save for your children's education or pay off your mortgage early? Or, very commonly, should you buy an investment property or pay off your mortgage? Max out your retirement savings or pay off maxed-out credit cards? When there are so many priorities competing for your attention, it can seem impossible to focus on your top money goals.

We all have great dreams and goals but you need to be realistic, understand your limitations and prioritise what you spend your time and money on.

So just how do you prioritise? The definition of prioritise is 'to arrange according to priority.' Duh! Clearly we need to have a good think about what is really important and then rank in order of importance. This comes down to you, and your priorities – which will be different to others, I'm sure!

You set priorities every day; priorities about what tasks will be done for the day, week or even month. For some reason long-term priorities get placed in the too hard basket because – why? They're too far away? Just because they are not urgent doesn't mean they are not important.

Successful prioritising is all about balancing that which is urgent and that which is important. Urgent stuff that's not done has adverse consequences whereas important work undone will probably have longer-term consequences. The point I'm making is that both need to be put into your schedule of things to do.

Let me explain by way of examples from a financial planner's point of view:

Important. If you want to create wealth, it's extremely important to purchase an investment property but it's not urgent.

Important and urgent. Your family needs to be protected. If you don't have any insurance cover then this is top of the list. Get some!

My main message is that your finances need to be prioritised and tackled one at a time. Your financial planner will assist you in putting together your financial plan. Go prepared though with a list of the things you think are important to you and have a conversation with your partner about this so you're both in agreement.

Do you love me just
because my daddy
left me a fortune?

Not at all, darling.
I would love you no
matter who left you
the money!

CHAPTER 12:
Estate planning

What is Estate Planning?

You've heard the saying 'where there's a will there's a way?' Well when it comes to estate planning 'where there's a will, there's a relative!' Estate planning is an integral part of the financial planning process, yet all too often estate planning is seen as simply having a Will. However, it is far more complex than this – involving family structures and beneficiaries, as well as powers of attorney, trusts, taxation issues and potentially, business succession, guardianship provisions and superannuation and insurance arrangements.

The aim of estate planning is to ensure that the right assets are transferred to the appropriate people at the appropriate time. The importance of estate planning within the context of an overall financial plan has increased over the past decade. The ageing population and the government's push for a self-funded retirement have led to an increasing need for quality advice and guidance on estate planning issues. Not only do financial planners need to advise those passing the wealth on, but also those receiving the wealth, i.e. the beneficiaries.

The emotional point to make is that a good Will which covers most of the below will keep your relatives out of court; it will ensure that they're not left with complicated messes to clean up and that they can all carry on with their lives – with happy memories of you!

When developing an estate plan, the following components need to be considered:

1. A Will that incorporates testamentary trusts
2. Powers of attorney
3. Advanced health directives on death and incapacitation
4. Superannuation and insurance nominations
5. Business succession agreement

Clear? Probably not, so it's best to speak to a professional who can ensure you cover all the things that are important to you and that will make sure your loved ones are properly taken care of without stress and complications after you're gone.

So what assets are included in the Will?

A Will only deals with assets that are owned by the testator (the deceased) in his or her own right. Only these can be passed on via the estate. Rather than providing you with a list of what will be included in the Will, let's look at which assets will not form part of the Will:

- Properties which are held jointly with someone else
- Assets held in a family trust
- Assets owned by a company
- Superannuation death benefit proceeds
- Life insurance policy proceeds owned by someone else or another entity
- Life interests

Each of these areas need to addressed separately in dealing with your estate planning needs. Your affairs are probably quite complex. You may have a holiday house, assets in various trusts or companies and complicated financial arrangements that have grown over the years. Therefore you need to take the time to sit down with your financial planner, solicitor and accountant at the same time to map out what needs to be done. If you do it all at the same time, you get it over and done with. Your goal is the best possible outcome for your estate.

What is an executor and what is their role?

The executor of your estate is the person who executes the instructions in your Will. The role is one of trust as well as one that comes with great responsibility. This means your decision needs to take into account your executor's abilities and probably needs to be someone with some sort of expertise. If the estate is complex with various ownership arrangements, then it would be prudent to appoint someone with proven business and accounting skills. Alternatively, if it is a simple estate, then perhaps a trusted friend may be appropriate.

A good executor will ideally be someone who is willing and able to undertake the role and is likely to survive the testator. Other factors include:

- geographical closeness
- knowledge of the type of assets within the estate
- honesty and high level of integrity
- impartiality between beneficiaries
- knowledge and willingness to seek expert advice when needed.

Estate planning for blended families

Demographic trends such as divorce rates; second marriages and relationship trends have seen an increase in the number of alternative family structures such as step and blended families. While the term 'blended family' may invoke images of a wine and roses 'Brady Bunch', real life is often far more complex and challenging. The reality is these can create some significant estate planning issues for clients.

Financial advisers and other advice providers who work with blended families need to be aware of the estate planning issues that can arise, as well as practical strategies that may be employed to help ease or even prevent potential difficulties. If you have a blended family, understand that you need a new mind-set to deal with the issues and that you need an adviser with experience in this area. Ask the simple question of your adviser, "Have you dealt with this situation before, and what are the issues I need to consider?"

Here comes the challenge – potential challenges to a Will

Each state and territory in Australia has implemented laws that enable people to contest Wills. If someone feels they have a legitimate expectation of consideration by the testator (you) to challenge the Will and have been left out of a Will or were not adequately provided for, they have the right to contest. It is essential that you demonstrate that you have considered all spouses, children and other family members, as well as close friends and other potential dependants in making the provisions of your Will.

There are many ways to achieve this, such as establishing a detailed memorandum which effectively means that if a Will is challenged, the deceased can still have their say in court and state the reasons why their decisions were made.

Needless to say if you believe there might be the possibility of a challenge to the Will, it is best to try and diffuse this early in the estate planning process while you're still alive.

Another complication might also arise as a result of multiple marriages, stepchildren and unbalanced distribution of assets. If you want to favour one child over another, once again a letter could be written into the estate plan that explains the reasons why the decision was made.

Who can challenge a Will?

The following people are generally able to challenge a Will in Australia's states and territories, depending on the law applicable in that jurisdiction:

- A spouse of the deceased
- A former spouse of the deceased
- Children of the deceased
- A person who is divorced from the deceased but who at the time of death is entitled to receive maintenance from the deceased
- A person who at any time was dependent on the deceased including a member of the same household as the deceased, or dependants who lived in the same household

The fact that a person is able to bring a challenge against a Will does not mean they will win such a challenge. The court must take into consideration the moral obligation of the deceased to provide for the claimant against the competing moral duty to provide for other beneficiaries under the Will. In other words the court will try to decide what is fair from the facts presented to it. If a challenge is successful, the court has the power to change how the estate will be distributed.

Whether a claim is successful or not, it is the estate that will generally pay the legal costs. As they say, the only winners in a bitter divorce or a contested Will are the lawyers – and you don't want that. The point here is to think it all through now, while you have all your marbles, while you're alive and while you can impact the outcome. Ultimately, the estate itself may reduce in value because people are fighting each other – lawyers generally only get involved because someone has died and not thought about the estate planning issues for themselves, their children, their spouse, or issues pertaining to any potential claim by an ex-spouse, a former spouse. Sure, it's not a cheerful exercise, but it's better than giving lawyers truckloads of your hard earned.

So what action needs to be taken after death?

When a person dies with their Will in place, the main estate planning duties rest with the executor nominated in the Will.

Essentially, the executor's role is to carry out duties in accordance with the Will (and any relevant laws that apply). This includes:

- locating the Will
- determining the assets of the estate
- paying any debts and liabilities
- distributing assets to beneficiaries named in the Will
- managing assets such as trusts and property for a period of time. This might involve attending shareholder or body corporate meetings for assets held
- possibly holding assets for a period of time (e.g. for children until they reach adulthood).

Paying for the funeral

The first task that the executor needs to do involves locating the original Will and immediately checking what provisions have been made for a person's funeral. A number of people prefer to make their funeral arrangements before death so that the expense and emotional impact isn't borne by family and friends of the deceased. Some people even set aside up to $10,000 so that a nice wake can be held to celebrate the passing. The first thing to do is to get the Will and have a look at those particular wishes.

Estate planning checklist

It's likely that a number of organisations/people will need to be informed once a person has died, as debts might need to be resolved. It's a good idea to prepare a checklist of these people and organisations during the estate planning process, as it will help to reduce any hassles when the testator dies. The checklist is likely to identify:

- executor of the estate
- professionals such as a solicitor and accountant
- church/religious institutions
- pension/annuity providers
- banks, building societies, credit unions
- investment institutions, fund managers and stockbrokers
- general insurers and life insurers
- debtors
- motor vehicle registry
- utilities companies (e.g. electricity, gas, water, phone)
- family doctor
- local council for rates notices, etc.
- employers and employees
- club and association memberships
- Centrelink or Department of Veterans' Affairs.

'Money, if it does not bring you happiness, will at least help you be miserable in comfort.'

HELEN GURLEY BROWN

CHAPTER 13: Superannuation

Super seems to be one of those subjects that turns people off. Maybe because it's so far in the future? Who knows? But it's another of those 'set it up well now, forget about it' things. There is lots of information about superannuation, in books or on the internet, whether from government organisations or major corporations. I'll try to give a potted selection of the things you need to know below. For people like me who are involved in superannuation in their day-to-day work, many of the rules and principles seem obvious.

One problem for members (you) of super funds is that the rules have changed over time – so you're probably now a little confused, you may have snippets of information that seem at odds with what you thought was happening, or you may have just zoned out.

So rather than flood you with even more information, let me take a different tact and introduce you to some information you may not know. We've already covered an important one in the previous chapter namely that super will not automatically be dealt with by a Will. Here are a few others.

12 things you may not know about super

1. Superannuation is not an investment

Superannuation is not itself an investment – rather, it is a vehicle designed to make investing for retirement more attractive by limiting the amount of tax that is paid within the fund. It is therefore simply a tax structure.

Subject to certain rules, a super fund can invest in virtually any of the assets that a member could invest in personally. Most super funds offer members a choice of how they invest. These can range from conservative options invested mostly in cash and fixed interest to highly aggressive options invested exclusively in shares and property.

The media may add to the confusion about super fund performance results with headlines such as 'Super gets returns of 15%' or 'Your super goes backwards'. The inference is that all super funds are the same, which is not the case. Usually, the media is talking about balanced funds in super, often the default investment option when members make no choice themselves. However, even balanced funds are not all the same. The balanced option in one fund may have 70% invested in growth assets, whereas the balanced option in another fund may have only 50% invested in growth assets.

2. Superannuation is not for everyone
Superannuation gets 'talked up' so much that the implication is often that everyone should have super. In fact being forced to have super, particularly those on lower incomes, disadvantages some people. Let me explain.

Employer and other concessional contributions are taxed at 15% in super, and investment earnings are taxed at 15%. Capital gains in super are effectively taxed at 10% where relevant assets are held by the fund for at least 12 months.

A person earning a taxable income of $44,000 will have an effective tax rate of less than 15% when the low income tax offset (LITO) is considered. Compare this to the 15% tax that applies in the super environment and it's clear super is not a good strategy, tax wise.

3. Superannuation guarantee is paid quarterly
One of the potential drawbacks of the superannuation guarantee (SG) is that an employee does not need to take any action to receive it. Their employer arranges it all. Because of this, it is easy for an employee to forget it. If the employee earned $50,000 a year, the SG would be $4,500. If this amount were included in their pay, they certainly wouldn't forget it.

The SG is calculated every payday by an employer as 9.25% (increasing to 12% by 2019) of 'ordinary time earnings'. The employer is required to pay the SG contributions for each financial quarter into super by the 28th day of the following month (except for the December quarter when they have until 28 February).

Employees should confirm that their employer is calculating the SG correctly and that the contributions are recorded on their annual benefit statement.

4. Contribution caps are an individual's responsibility

There must be some limit on the tax concessional super available to any individual, otherwise many would take unfair advantage and our tax system would start to fail, with an unfair burden faced by those who couldn't afford to divert funds into super.

Before 1 July 2007:

- The Australian Taxation Office (ATO) monitored reasonable benefit limits (RBLs).
- Employers monitored the deductible contributions that were paid in a year.
- There are limits (caps) on concessional (tax deductible) contributions and on non-concessional (after tax) contributions. The caps apply:
- for each tax year
- for each individual
- for all applicable contributions to all super funds.

Contributions over the caps are subject to excess contributions tax – effectively 46.5%.

No one (with the possible exception of a financial planner) monitors whether the member is at risk of exceeding the caps. It is the member's own responsibility and they will usually only discover the extra tax six to nine months after the end of the tax year.

The good news is that super was reviewed and in the 2013 Budget it was announced that the government will scrap the excess contributions tax and that it will slightly increase the contributions cap. At the time of writing it is yet to become law and given there was a change in government in September 2013 time will tell whether it's ultimately implemented.

5. Up to age 65, anyone can have super

In the past, superannuation was only for the employed. The restrictions on who can contribute to super have been relaxed over the years and from 2004, anyone under 65 (whether they are employed or not) has been able to put money into super.

This provides good opportunities:

- for members who are no longer working to put extra money into super before starting an income stream
- for people without super to put inheritances or other windfalls in a tax advantaged structure.

6. Tax in super can be less than 15%

Superannuation funds pay tax at a flat 15% on all their assessable income. This includes concessional (tax deductible) contributions and investment earnings such as interest, rent and dividends. In practice, most super funds pay tax at less than 15%.

- For an asset held more than 12 months, the capital gain when the asset is disposed of is discounted by a third – effectively reducing the tax rate to 10%.

- Funds can claim a tax deduction for the expenses of running the fund as well as the premiums for life, total and permanent disablement (TPD) and income protection insurance cover.
- Dividends paid by Australian companies can carry a tax credit under the dividend imputation rules. The credit can be up to 30% (the company tax rate) and can be used to offset tax payable by the super fund. For example, if the tax credit was large enough it could eliminate the tax on concessional contributions paid by the fund.

Statistics released by the Australian Prudential Regulation Authority (APRA) indicate that most members remain in the default balanced investment option in large super funds. A balanced fund usually has 25 to 35% invested in Australian shares and so the imputation credits and other tax concessions on those shares could reduce the effective tax rate of the fund to less than 10%.

7. Life insurance in super can be tax effective

On the death of an individual, life insurance provides a lump sum to pay off debts and support dependants and it can provide capital for other purposes. Life insurance can be arranged privately or through a super fund.

The advantages of having life insurance in super are:

- The size of the super fund may allow it to negotiate cheaper premiums with a life insurer.
- A set amount of cover may be provided (called automatic acceptance) without the need for medical examinations or health checks.
- The super fund can claim the premiums as a tax deduction, thereby reducing the cost to the member.

- Premiums are deducted from the member's account so there is less chance of the policy lapsing because premiums are not paid on time.
- The member can make salary sacrifice contributions to pay the premiums, so premiums are paid in pre-tax dollars.
- Benefits paid to tax dependants are tax free with no maximum limit.

Many super funds will allow the member to buy extra life insurance, though this is likely to require a more detailed underwriting process. There are also circumstances where holding life insurance privately would be a better arrangement. This is an area where a skilled planner can help.

8. Super funds will (sometimes) pay out before retirement

While super is for retirement, there are circumstances when it can be paid out (in full or in part) before retirement.

Obvious (though undesirable) examples are:

- death
- total and permanent disablement (called invalidity in super-speak)
- diagnosis of terminal illness.

Other examples are:

- Financial hardship: to release money in this way requires the member to have been receiving Centrelink benefits and to be unable to pay bills.

- On compassionate grounds: to release money in this way requires the member (or their immediate family) to have significant medical expenses, to have funeral expenses, or to be at risk of foreclosure on their home mortgage.
- Unrestricted non-preserved benefits: when the current preservation rules were introduced in 1999, some members had money in their super that they could have accessed immediately in cash. This amount was quarantined and can still be accessed at any time (though tax may be payable depending on their age and the amount involved).
- Once the member reaches preservation age (currently 55) they can access their super as a 'transition to retirement' pension.

These are legitimate ways for the member to gain access to their super. The super regulators are concerned about schemes where members access their super early and illegally. Promoters of such schemes have had legal action taken against them and members have had tax penalties imposed on them.

9. Super is tax free from age 60, but retirement comes first

When the major super changes came into effect from 1 July 2007, the headlines said 'Super is free from age 60'. Some members misinterpreted this to mean that they could claim their super tax-free at age 60. To be able to access super as a lump sum, a member must satisfy a 'condition of release'. Usually this will mean they have satisfied a Superannuation Industry (Supervision) Act 1993 (SIS Act) retirement definition. The three definitions are:

- To have reached age 65
- To have left a job after age 60. This can be any genuine position of gainful employment. It does not have to be the person's main job.
- To have reached preservation age (currently 55) and have declared an intention to never work again. The member can change their mind and return to work but if they abuse the rule there may be tax penalties.

10. Super can be left to grow after age 65

Until May 2006, members were required to 'use their super' at age 65 unless they were still working. They also had to use their super at age 75 even if they were still working. 'Use their super' meant to start an income stream or take the money as a lump sum out of the concessionally taxed super structure.

This so called 'compulsory cashing' rule has since been abolished. Members can access their super when they satisfy a condition of release. However, the only time their super must be paid out is on death. This creates new opportunities for members, including:

- Retaining money in super as part of an estate planning strategy. However, members should be aware of the potential tax on death benefits paid to non-dependants.
- Saving extra money in super as a source of capital to pay for medical expenses or aged care.

Members should bear in mind that where super accounts are in the accumulation phase they do not attract the same tax-free status as those in pension phase, i.e. being used to pay a pension to the member.

11. A pension can carry on after death

When an individual dies, the social security age pension for that person stops. If they have a partner, their age pension will increase to the higher single person's rate – but this is less than the combined age pension received by a couple. The surviving pensioner will be subject to the single person's income and asset tests so they may not receive the maximum pension.

Some guaranteed pensions paid by super funds (and annuities) will continue to pay out after the death of the primary pensioner. They will usually pay a reduced pension to a person nominated as the 'reversionary' beneficiary.

Allocated and account-based pensions paid by super funds can also nominate a reversionary. In this case:

- The reversionary must be a dependant of the primary pensioner – a spouse, child under 18 or someone who is financially dependent on, or in an interdependent relationship with, the deceased.
- A pension payable to a child can only continue until the child reaches age 25 and must then be cashed out.
- The new pensioner chooses the amount of income to be paid by the pension and the way the funds are invested.

12. Superannuation is more than just a retirement nest egg

The 'compare the pair' advertisements on TV oversimplify super. Super is portrayed as being nothing more than an investment and that the fund with the lowest fees will generate the largest retirement benefit. There is much more to super – in terms of investment choices, taxation and things like life insurance and more.

A good adviser can tailor a super fund to suit the current and future needs of a client as part of a complete financial plan. For example, the adviser could:

- recommend an appropriate fund
- recommend an appropriate amount of life, TPD and income protection cover
- recommend contribution strategies to maximise tax benefits
- identify tax traps, such as excessive contributions tax
- recommend appropriate long-term investments
- develop target retirement benefits and strategies to attain them
- ensure death benefits align with the client's estate plan.

The changes to super legislation, although thankfully not regular, are a good reason why super isn't completely set and forget. A good adviser can keep you abreast of the changes, including product changes, and ensure you're taking full advantage of any changes. And hopefully, after reading this book you'll understand why a good adviser makes sense and you'll choose one who can maximise all your financial arrangements.

Remember the
golden rule:

Those who have the
gold make the rules.

CHAPTER 14:
Self-managed
super funds

SMSFs are like a V8 – plenty of power under the bonnet that can really propel your strategy and wealth forward but it is expensive to run. There are fees to set up the account, annual ASIC fees, annual accounting fees, annual audit fees – everyone gets a shot at you. But, should you have enough funds to justify an SMSF, the different products available to you can be advantageous.

There are question marks. Who does what? What does the accountant do and what does the adviser do – everyone will blame each other if something goes wrong.

What about insurance and how to fund loan payouts upon the death of a member – does the money go to a dependent member's account and so on?

There is the issue of TPD within super. When you take out TPD Insurance there is the possibility of a payout if you are unable to perform the duties of your 'own' occupation or 'any' occupation. Naturally the 'any' definition is very broad and you really would have to be pretty disabled to meet that definition whereas being unable to perform the duties of your own occupation is an easier definition to meet.

The problem arises when you have TPD within super and make a claim. You may meet the 'own' occupation definition of the insurance company, however, by law, you can only get the money out of super if you are unable to perform the duties of 'any' occupation. This is the definition under current superannuation law. Good advice is imperative!

Self-Managed Super

Do-it-Yourself (DIY) super via a self-managed super fund (SMSF) is becoming an increasingly popular choice for investors who want to have control of how their superannuation monies are invested. However, if you are thinking of leaving your current fund to get better returns or other benefits from your own DIY fund, make sure you discuss your options in detail with your financial planner. The grass isn't always greener and your new choices are just as prone to market fluctuations as your old ones may have been – if that's why you are leaving.

There's a lot more to an SMSF than you might think and the penalties for doing the wrong thing can be as severe as a jail term. Still interested? Read on...

What is an SMSF?

An SMSF is a super fund with up to four members who can accumulate future retirement benefits. In most cases, all members of an SMSF must be trustees of the fund or directors of the fund's corporate trustee. A good adviser will help you with the set-up documentation and walk through your obligations. Essentially, you want to be rather good at record keeping and keep an eye on the annual accounting obligations. The Superannuation Industry (Supervision) Act 1993 and Regulations (SIS) and related legislation govern Australian super funds and the Australian Taxation Office (ATO) is responsible for overseeing the regulation of SMSFs.

Why establish an SMSF?

The three key reasons for establishing your own SMSF are control, flexibility and investment choice. You (the trustee) decide on your fund's investment strategy and choose what your fund invests in. Set up properly, the fund can even invest in assets as diverse as art and property. If you rather enjoy this aspect – getting involved in the selection of assets process – then you might quite enjoy the whole SMSF process.

Additionally, like all super funds, an SMSF receives concessional tax treatment. The top tax rate for the investment earnings of your SMSF is 15% – probably well below the top tax rate applicable to your own income.

It's important to note that this tax concession is only available where you operate a 'complying fund' – that is an SMSF that complies with all the rules set out by SIS and the ATO.

The key areas of compliance for an SMSF relate to:

- meeting the sole purpose test
- documenting an investment strategy and investing in line with it
- prohibition on financial assistance to members and their relatives (you can't lend funds to yourself or relatives)
- in-house asset rules
- conducting all transactions at arm's length
- prohibition against borrowing with certain exceptions
- acquisition of assets from related parties (designed to stop people 'buying' assets at inflated prices from relatives etc.).

What are my responsibilities?

Investment strategy

The technical definition is as follows: In accordance with the Superannuation Industry (Supervision) Act 1993 (the SIS Act), the trustees of every complying superannuation fund, including SMSFs, must formulate and give effect to an investment strategy that will have regard to the 'whole of the circumstances' of the fund members. In plain English; you must have a good investment strategy that helps you create wealth for your retirement income. Your adviser can do this for you.

Given the predictions that almost one and a half trillion dollars will be held in SMSFs by 2021 and the share of total superannuation assets held in SMSFs is expected to be one third of this amount, the way in which the investment strategies of SMSFs are devised and implemented is becoming increasingly important in achieving the retirement goals of many Australians.

This is not something to undertake lightly – the penalties can be severe and you are talking about the assets that will carry your retirement! Get a good financial planner to assist.

Sole purpose test

Under superannuation legislation a complying superannuation fund exists for the sole purpose of providing benefits for members upon their retirement. The sole purpose test aims to ensure that funds are invested in a way that minimises risk and, as far as possible, secures the members' benefits for their retirement.

The ATO regards failure to comply with the sole purpose test as the most serious material breach of the legislation and such a breach can lead to the loss of the fund's complying status and tax concessions (half of the fund can go to tax!), and can also incur other civil and criminal penalties.

Buying property within an SMSF

Borrowing within SMSFs

A change to the SIS Act effective 24 September 2007, enabled superannuation funds, including SMSFs, to borrow using a type of loan structure with limited recourse. SMSFs can now borrow to invest, provided the SMSF trustee borrows the money in accordance with an arrangement with the following features:

- The borrowing is used to acquire an asset.
- The asset is held on trust so that the SMSF trustee receives a beneficial interest and a right to acquire the legal ownership of the asset (or any replacement) through the payment of instalments. (By paying off the loan, the superfund eventually owns the asset outright. For example, an investment property.)
- The lender's recourse against the SMSF trustee in the event of default on the borrowing and related fees, or the exercise of rights by the SMSF trustee, is limited to rights relating to the asset. (The bank can't access other superfund assets if you default on the loan for whatever reason.)

- The asset (or any replacement) must be one that the SMSF trustee is permitted to acquire or hold directly.

While an SMSF member can now lend money to his or her own super fund, it must be for the sole purpose of providing retirement benefits for members, conducted on an arm's length basis, and comparable to what a financial institution would provide regarding the terms and rate of interest offered.

Property investments

Property investment, particularly geared investments, may be particularly appealing to some investors. However, limited funds in an SMSF, combined with the fund's inability to borrow (with the exception of the use of instalment warrants), may mean that property investment is not appropriate.

Investing a large proportion of the fund's money in property may also cause difficulty with regard to the fund's liquidity, e.g. if there is a need to make an unexpected benefit pay-out.

For these reasons, you may be better off holding property investments personally, rather than through your SMSF.

If you are going to borrow to purchase property in your SMSF then the diagram below shows how it should be structured. Make sense? No? Don't blame you but it's the ATO who has specified this structure for such a purchase. You need to have this set up by a financial planner who has extensive knowledge in this specialised space and you need to understand it. Why do you need to remember it? Because the ATO has never accepted ignorance as an excuse!

Wealth Creation

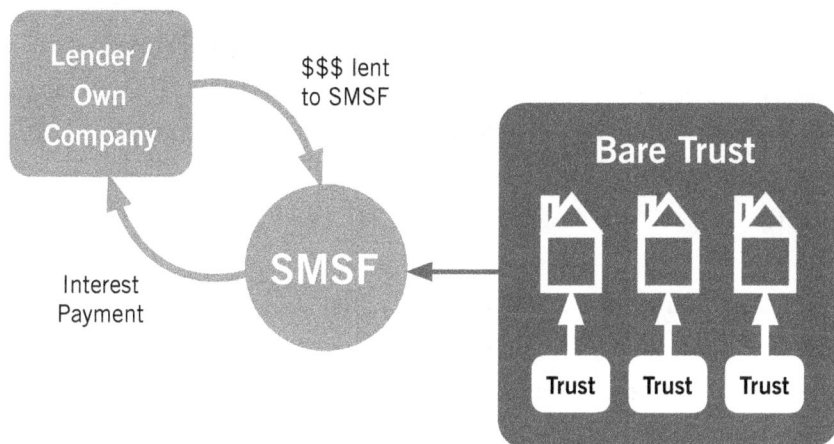

Is an SMSF for you?

According to ASIC, there are four key questions when considering whether an SMSF is right for a client.

1. Is the fund strictly for retirement benefits only (otherwise known as the sole purpose test)?
2. Does the client have the time and skills to manage their own superannuation, establish an investment strategy, select investments and fulfil the responsibilities as the trustee?
3. Will the benefits be worth the costs?
4. How will switching to an SMSF affect the client's current superannuation, including insurances within super?

ASIC figures suggest that if a client has less than $150,000 to $200,000 in superannuation, it may not be worthwhile establishing an SMSF, purely because of the cost involved, estimated to be approximately $2,000 to $5,000 per year. ATO data shows that approximately 30% of SMSFs currently hold less than $200,000 in assets. Why oh why are clients listening to advisers who only have their own interests at heart!

Here's how to work out if an SMSF is for you

The first step in the process for establishing an SMSF is determining the appropriateness of this structure for you. The main points you need to understand are:

- cost
- your level of financial literacy
- your needs, and
- the availability of time and resources for managing the fund.

How much will it cost?

Firstly, consider whether you have sufficient funds to justify the cost of running an SMSF – with average establishment costs running from several hundred dollars to more than $1,000 and on-going costs from $2,000 pa, you need a substantial existing superannuation balance and/or significant on-going contributions to justify the on-going expenses of running your own fund.

In the Australian Securities & Investments Commission (ASIC) publication 'Is self managed super right for you?', they suggest that a person would need around $200,000 in superannuation to make the costs of an SMSF worthwhile. You will also require a reasonable level of financial literacy to appreciate and carry out your obligations as trustee.

There are benefits to doing it though!

An SMSF is an ideal structure to implement higher level planning strategies such as combining salary sacrificing and re-contributions; as a family wealth creation and protection vehicle, and for estate planning.

Can you manage?

Finally, your capacity to manage the fund must also be considered. Even where an administrator or accountant is appointed to manage the fund's administrative requirements, trustees must hold and document all meetings regarding the fund's activities, prepare and monitor the fund's investment strategy, and ensure that the fund remains compliant under the law. Of course, most advisers can assist with this in terms of document templates and so on.

Ultimately the trustees of the fund are legally responsible for the fund, regardless of the extent to which superannuation professionals and administrators may assist to reduce the day-to-day administrative burden. Again, ignorance is no excuse!

The Australian Taxation Office (ATO) has produced a number of publications that can help you decide if an SMSF is for you. Have a good chat to your adviser and then read the booklets he or she gives you so that you really do understand the obligations and the workload coming your way. The guide entitled, 'Does SMSF suit me?' can be accessed online at www.ato.gov.au and covers many of the issues outlined above. Copies of the booklets entitled, 'Guide for SMSF Trustees – Role and responsibilities of trustees – Operating a Self Managed Superannuation Fund' (NAT11032) and 'DIY super – it's your money... but not yet!' (NAT11393) can be ordered from the ATO – just go to their website.

Trustee responsibilities

A trustee is charged with the responsibility of managing a fund. As the trustees of an SMSF are effectively the fund's members as well, and the purpose of an SMSF is to provide retirement benefits for members, the trustees must follow all rules and regulations to ensure retirement benefits are preserved. In other words, you're one and the same person; make sure you get it right.

There are four major steps involved in establishing an SMSF:

1. Establish a trust, and obtain a trust deed (your adviser can assist)
2. Elect to be a regulated fund, obtain a tax file number and an Australian business number (ABN) for the fund (again, adviser can handle this)
3. Prepare an investment strategy (adviser will assist based on conversations with you and your risk profile)
4. Open a bank account (easy!)

While an accountant or financial planner can, and often does assist in having these tasks carried out on a trustee's behalf, the responsibility for ensuring they have been completed correctly still rests with the trustee. This is true of all functions within an SMSF, with the exception of auditing.

The responsibilities of a trustee include:

- making sure the sole purpose test is met so that you and your fellow members enjoy a great retirement
- preparing and implementing an investment strategy, and making investment decisions that fall within the bounds of superannuation and tax laws
- accepting contributions and paying pension or lump sum benefits in accordance with superannuation and tax laws
- ensuring an approved auditor is appointed for each income year
- undertaking administrative tasks such as lodging annual returns and record keeping

- making sure new trustees sign the trustee declaration.
- In most of the above your adviser will ensure you're properly advised on how to carry out these functions. This is why it's imperative that you find a good, experienced adviser who you trust to help you in a proficient manner.

The law says:

Further, the Superannuation Industry (Supervision) Act 1993 (SIS Act) requires trustees to:

- act honestly in all matters concerning their fund
- exercise the same degree of care, skill and diligence as an ordinary prudent person in managing their fund
- act in the best interest of all fund beneficiaries
- keep the money and assets of their fund separate from other money and assets (for example, personal assets)
- retain control over their fund
- not enter into contracts or behave in a way that hinders trustees from performing or exercising their functions or powers
- allow members access to certain information

Get it wrong – what happens?

Failure to meet these requirements may result in: a fund being made a non-complying fund and losing its tax concessions; disqualification as a trustee; and prosecution or the imposition of civil and criminal penalties. If a trustee fails to act in accordance with a fund's trust deed, other affected members may also take legal action against that particular trustee.

Outsourcing functions

Given that many trustees will not have sufficient skill in all areas of fund operation and compliance, areas may be outsourced, including accounting, production of financial statements and administration. Auditing of an SMSF must be outsourced to an approved auditor. Your accountant will help with most of this or your financial adviser will be able to package this up for you.

Investment management is another area that is generally outsourced to an adviser who can assist trustees in making investment decisions. What he or she will do is make a series of recommendations based on your risk profile. What you need to do is ensure those recommendations are truly for your benefit, and not because they earn the adviser a better commission than the other options. Legislation has taken care of this to some extent, but do ask the 'independence' question.

For all outsourcing arrangements, it is advisable to have a written agreement in place outlining the terms and scope of the relationship. Most advisers and accountants will do this automatically. Be aware though, that while your accountant and adviser will undoubtedly fulfil the tasks they're asked to do, you, as Trustee, have to take ultimate responsibility for the operation of a fund.

Responsibilities of advisers and accountants

While both advisers and accountants have a role in working with their clients in managing SMSFs, be aware that accountants are generally not licensed to give financial advice (that is, where they do not hold an Australian Financial Services Licence (AFSL)). This means the lines of responsibility both at the outset and during the life of the SMSF can be blurry.

Advisers and accountants must both ensure that they remain completely up to date with the various pieces of legislation covering SMSFs – the SIS Act, the Corporations Act and taxation legislation.

'The trick is to stop thinking of it as 'your' money.'

TAX AUDITOR

CHAPTER 15:
Is Now A Good Time To Invest?

A lot of people worry about investing – what happens if I lose all my money? What happens if there's another financial disaster? It will happen; the trick is to prepare for it. Here's some analysis about what happened and what are the lessons are for 'Joe Average' SMSF investor.

GFC – Wait for the next one!

The first signs of distress in financial markets emerged around the middle of 2007 when two funds related to US financial company Bear Stearns announced serious problems with their holdings of mortgage-backed securities (MBS).

These signs turned into tremors as they ebbed and flowed over subsequent months, intensifying in March 2008 when Bear Stearns effectively collapsed and was rescued by JP Morgan. The financial crisis then reached its zenith in September 2008 when US securities company Lehman Brothers went into bankruptcy, and the large insurance company AIG was rescued by the US Government along with the two large mortgage agencies, Fannie Mae and Freddie Mac.

The Lehman bankruptcy saw many parts of global financial markets almost come to a complete halt and fears arose about the stability of the global financial system. Governments and central banks responded to these developments with a large and wide-ranging policy response, including sizeable fiscal stimulus, large reductions in policy interest rates, guarantees of bank deposits and bank debt issuance, and in some cases, sizeable government ownership of troubled financial institutions.

Even though it appears the GFC is almost gone and I stress almost, if you're an investor and you hang around long enough, I guarantee you will experience another downturn. You will experience your shares or property values go down dramatically. But keep things in perspective, as the reason they are coming down is because they have had a great run up.

To paraphrase, "What goes up must come down." The good thing is that there are more ups than downs, which means that over the long-term asset values rise.

Humans have this innate ability to recover from adversity, pick ourselves up and move on. We are relatively optimistic as a whole. After all we have gone through two world wars and in 1929 a massive world depression, so there's every reason to expect that there would be a recovery from any recession (unless it's the end of the world in which case it doesn't matter anyway).

Impact and lessons for Australia?

According to The Year Book Australia 2009-10 (ABS) 21 January 2013, if you're an economist you'll probably say that the most important lesson is that investors should take a long-term view. Most financial planners would probably say that one of the main lessons was a greater understanding of risk.

The Reserve Bank of Australia (Phillip Lowe, the Bank's assistant governor) outlines three main lessons:

1. Flexibility
2. Appropriate regulation
3. Resilience in the financial markets

The World Bank in its Global Economic Prospects 2010 document says, "The lessons of the financial crisis are likely to shape financial policies and market reactions for some time to come. Beyond the immediate and unprecedented global recession that it has provoked, the crisis can be expected to alter the global financial landscape significantly over the next five to 15 years."

Back to basics

Despite the market uncertainty, I stand by the traditional approach to asset allocation, which is that a financial planner should remain focused on solid foundations, which take into account a client's:

- risk profile
- goals and objectives
- investment timeframe.

It is crucial that planners listen to a client's attitude towards these issues. To build a portfolio that matches key objectives with the appropriate assets, the planner should be asking themself, "What does my client want to achieve and how comfortable are they with the level of risk undertaken to get them there?"

Although the global financial crisis has caused many clients to be concerned about the state of their investments, it doesn't mean that financial advisers were necessarily wrong in the decisions made around asset allocation, provided that a client's risk profile, objectives and investment timeframe were taken into consideration. However, the crisis does highlight the need to ensure that client portfolios are properly allocated to withstand market volatility. You might like to consider some 'rebalancing' of your own portfolio. There may be certain cases where exposure to specific product groups within asset classes will need to be changed; however, the exposure to the overall asset class should not necessarily change unless your situation has changed.

It is impossible to time the market. As the saying goes, "No one rings the bell when the recovery is happening, and no one rings the bell when the market reaches its top".

It has taken some time for the turmoil to ease and the global financial and banking systems to recapitalise. But we seem to be almost at the end of the tunnel.

Market turbulence causes investors to move away from assets such as emerging market equities, private equity and alternative investments. Instead there has been a return to more traditional portfolio allocations, consisting largely of Australian equities and, to a lesser extent, international equities. Is it time to change back? Talk to your adviser.

Media role and 'noise'

Because of the abundance of information from a variety of sources available to investors on a daily basis it is often the case that some of that information is either incorrect or has been misinterpreted.

Journalists are often accused of misinterpreting or skewing the facts in favour of a particular angle. Similarly, the data or key messages given to the media, perhaps through government or company press releases, might also be incorrect. Ultimately, this can lead to illogical conclusions being made by investors and the stakes are high for mistakes.

Even worse, the message from the media can change within a few hours. At home I have copies of two editions of The Herald-Sun from 2001. One is the morning edition and the other the afternoon edition (back when they ran two editions per day). The morning edition's cover page had the following words in large headlines: "Crash", "lost" and "billion" as a reference to the billions that were 'lost' on the market the day before. The cover has a photo of sad people looking up to who knows where and extremely worried at the "billions" they have lost. There are lots of down arrows referring to the drop in share prices. It shows BHP dropped 25.9c to $9.28. Interesting that eight years later (2008) the share price peaked at $48.74. That's a return of 500% in eight years, I'd take that!

Anyway, back to the media. As usually happens, there was a rebound in the markets that same morning (a substantial one I might add) and all the front page of the afternoon edition says (just in time for all the people catching the public transport on the way home) is "Rebound". Whilst true, it doesn't really excite anywhere near the magnitude of fear the previous heading created.

We all know that good news travels fast but bad news travels faster. We know that bad news (and headlines) sells much better than good news. All of which means you need to bear this in mind when reading the paper, watching TV programs or anything on the internet when it comes to financial information.

If you are going to read it, then please keep it all in perspective. Remember the share price of BHP? What do you think the share price will be in another eight years time? At a guess – probably higher than where it is currently.

Because there is a risk of the information being misinterpreted you need to ensure that you understand what you are reading and that you are reacting in the correct manner. You need to try to remain focused on your strategy and not be caught out by the spin of what may or may not happen.

Your financial planner can help you to filter out the noise by educating you about the goals of your investment strategy and, where relevant, emphasising the importance of a long-term investment approach, which should not necessarily alter due to volatility.

For instance, if you have 20 years until retirement and have invested in growth assets, you should not be spending too much time focusing on what your BHP shares are doing today or tomorrow.

Your planner plays a very important role, ensuring that you stay true to your strategy and making sure you don't lose focus on the end game.

Finally planners and clients must be willing to accept that there will always be noise and in the modern world, an abundance of information is just something we all have to get used to and work with to find the opportunities as they arise.

So while the GFC wasn't as hard for Australians compared to many other countries, the crisis still strongly reinforced investment basics. Know what you're investing in, including the risk/return trade-off. Get advice from a professional, be flexible, diversify and keep some capital in reserve. And what else? Oh yes, expect it to happen all over again at some stage in the future, just maybe not as bad.

Should I review my plans?
Ok it's now 12 months since a financial planner prepared a financial plan for you and gave you top advice. Just because you've implemented all his or her recommendations doesn't mean the process ends there. In fact, in many ways it's just beginning.

On-going financial planning reviews are an important part of ensuring that your financial plan remains relevant over time. The financial planning review process addresses changes to the following areas and adjusts your financial plan accordingly:

- your financial planning needs and objectives
- your income and expenditure
- your family situation and health
- your life insurance needs
- deductible and non-deductible debt
- the economic environment
- investment and superannuation portfolio performance
- your taxation position and any relevant changes in the current tax law
- any opportunities to reduce your tax payable
- social security issues
- new investment opportunities

While this is not a conclusive list, it gives you just a glimpse of what can change and what a financial planner can do for you when conducting on-going financial planning reviews. Ultimately, it's about having a trusted financial planner working with you over time to ensure that you are reaching your financial and life goals, and that you are doing it as efficiently and effectively as possible. Efficient in that it's working, and effective in that it's the right way to achieve your goals.

If we really did profit
from our mistakes,
I'd be extremely
rich by now.

CHAPTER 16:
Philanthropy

Give and you shall receive. It's karma right? Or in Christian terms the reference is "whatever you sow that's what you'll reap".

If you listen to all the magazines, commercials and advertisements, you'll probably conclude that the general philosophy on wealth is, "Get all you can; can all you get; then sit on the can."

Much is said or written about making money and enjoying it. There's nothing wrong with that. But I do believe strongly that we are to use our wealth in any way we can to assist the underprivileged and certainly the undernourished. We live in a very lucky country and are wealthier than something like 90 per cent of the world's population – yet because we all compare ourselves to our peer group and the people just slightly 'ahead' of us we often feel like we're doing it tough.

The past ten years have seen unprecedented growth in Australians giving to charitable causes. While many of these donations have been made on an unplanned or ad hoc basis in response to natural disasters and unexpected events such as the Boxing Day tsunami, Victorian bush-fires and Haitian earthquake, greater numbers of people want to give on a more planned or structured basis. This increase in philanthropy can be at least partly be attributed to the recent decade of economic prosperity, as well as changes to the tax system, which have both removed some disincentives to giving, and created a simpler structure for giving by individuals, families and businesses.

What is philanthropy?

Derived from a Greek word meaning 'the love of humanity', the term 'philanthropy' often conjures images of organised donations by wealthy individuals (or organisations) to charitable foundations or events. While Philanthropy Australia provides a formal definition as 'the planned or structured giving of money, time, goods and services or other to improve the well-being of humanity and the community', philanthropy is often more broadly used to describe any private action performed for public good. In this context, anyone can be a philanthropist, provided their actions or money are used for the good of society.

The Thoughts of Chairman Buffett

> "I'm having so much fun it's almost sinful."
> *Warren Buffet, Berkshire Hathaway AGM 2013.*

When I first heard this quote I thought, "Of course you're having fun Warren, you're a billionaire!" I could think of all the fun I'd have if I were a billionaire too. But rather than feeling envy I decided there was a lesson to be learnt. And that was to aim for wealth but at all times, to be content with what I have, be joyful and have plenty of fun along the way. How about you? Money isn't the be all and end all. Family is. Wealth is to make a good life for your family, to share a little with others and to enable the lifestyle you want in retirement. It's not a goal in itself.

In May 2013 Warren Buffett joined Twitter. My how the times they are a changing. In 1982, when Berkshire Hathaway hosted its first shareholder meeting, just 15 shareholders turned up. Back then, a single share of the holding company sold for just $1,000.

Today, a single share will set you back $162,000, and as the fortunes of the company have swelled, so have the numbers at its annual shareholder meeting.

At the annual AGM in May 2013, 35,000 investors flocked to Nebraska, to an event called by some the Woodstock of business. They came from far and wide to hear the insights of a man known as the 'Oracle of Omaha' – the chairman of Berkshire Hathaway, Warren Buffett.

Buffett, the world's best-known octogenarian businessman, took questions from investors – fans and critics – for close to six hours.

Amongst a host of other things, one thing he revealed which caught my eye was the following:

If you want to succeed, start having fun.

During the meeting, Buffett, along with his vice-chairman and long-time partner Charlie Munger, were asked what advice they would give to themselves 50 years ago.

"Find what turns you on," Buffett said.

He said both he and Munger started off working in a grocery store, but neither of them stayed there for long.

"We were lucky to be in this country to start with. But we found things we like to do very early in life and then we pushed very hard in doing those things. But we were enjoying it while we did it. We have had so much fun running Berkshire it's almost sinful. But we were lucky."

The message here is to find a career that you enjoy. Easier said than done of course, but the other upside to creating wealth is that you can build enough to enable the studies or whatever that get you in to another career. Yes! Even if you started off in a career you thought you had to do for money, you can change and you can achieve all your dreams. Maybe yours is to help others – creating wealth now is your passport to retiring early and being able to do just that.

After you've set up the platform for wealth creation that I'm talking about in this book, why not spend some time discovering what you find 'fun' to do as a career... and then set in place the steps that take you there.

Where to now?

Now that we've come to the end of the book can you tell me what is the ultimate wealth creation tool? Whenever I ask this question at speaking engagements there are numerous answers given in the room including:

- Property
- Shares
- Business
- Making money
- Robbing a bank (yes I've had that one).

So can you tell me which one is correct? The answer is none of them.

The ultimate wealth creation tool is a... wait for it... A PLAN! Yes that's right, a financial plan. So many people begin investing without any roadmap and then wonder why they are not on track or why things are getting tough.

A good financial plan should always have the following:

1. Your objectives
2. Inefficiencies
3. Recommendations
4. Investments
5. Insurance
6. Cash-Flow
7. Products

Off you go

The journey is now yours. Hopefully you know where to start, what to ask and how to assess your potential adviser. Let me recap very quickly.

- Have a plan
- Employ an independent financial planner
- Understand your risk profile – and that there is some risk
- Invest for the long-term
- Take out insurance and make a Will
- Consider DIY super if you're a 'details' person

And off course let me plug myself ... so if you want
to talk about your finances with a qualified, competent
and life loving financial planner then contact ME,
Ziggy on any of the following:

ziggy@peterziggy.com
www.peterziggy.com
0413 485 083

As a thank you to you the reader for purchasing this
book, I have additional free bonus material on my
website that you can access. Simply head over to
www.peterziggy.com click on the book logo for bonus
material and put in the code: MDGOT